14.95
D0265701

Implementing an Accounting System

The Financial Skills Series

The rapidly-changing role of the finance function in modern organisations is creating greater and more varied demands upon the skills of everyone involved in the world of finance and accounting. To enable busy professionals to keep up with this pace of change, Kogan Page has joined forces with the Chartered Institute of Management Accountants (CIMA) to create a lively, up-to-the-minute series of books on financial skills.

Highly practical in nature, each book is packed with expert advice and information on a specific financial skill, while the lively style adopted reflects the current dynamism of the discipline.

Already published in the series are:

Cost Control: A Strategic Guide
David Doyle
ISBN 0 7494 1167 8

Quality in the Finance Function
David Lynch
ISBN 0 7494 1145 7

Implementing an Accounting System
A Practical Guide
Revised Edition
Ray Franks
ISBN 0 7494 1052 3

While forthcoming books in the series include:

Strategic Financial Decisions
David Allen
ISBN 0 7494 1147 3

Investment Appraisal
A guide for Managers
Second Edition
Rob Dixon
ISBN 0 7494 1065 5

If you would like to be kept fully informed of new books in the series please contact the Marketing Department at Kogan Page, 120 Pentonville Road, London N1 9JN, *Tel* 071–278 0433, *Fax* 071–837 6348. CIMA members can also contact the Publishing Department at the Institute for further details of the series.

Implementing an Accounting System

A Practical Guide

REVISED EDITION

RAY
FRANKS

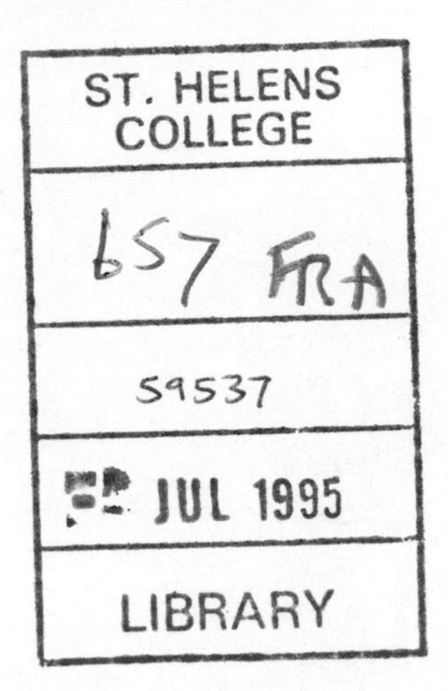

First published in 1990
Revised edition 1994

Kogan Page Limited
120 Pentonville Road
London N1 9JN

British Library Cataloguing in Publication Data

A CIP record for this book is available from the British Library.

ISBN 0 7494 1052 3

Typeset by Saxon Graphics Ltd
Printed and bound in Great Britain by Biddles Ltd, Guildford and Kings Lynn

CONTENTS

INTRODUCTION

1

The Importance of Accounting Systems

THE MYSTIQUE OF ACCOUNTING

It is no doubt of some solace to accountants that their discipline occasionally arouses as much fear of the unknown in others as, say, computing does in certain of their number. This feeling is still remarkably prevalent despite an ever greater emphasis being placed upon financial matters in the education and training of managers of many different persuasions. Part of the reason is no doubt a mystique which has been 'passed down' through many generations of business managers. Indeed, there is an old story which relates that, when the 'game' of business was invented, the captains of industry selected their teams and left some of the prospective players stamping their feet disconsolately on the sidelines. 'Never mind chaps' said one of the captains to the glum-faced onlookers, 'you can keep the score.' The story continues that, ever resentful of not having been selected to play, these unlucky and embittered people invented a method of scoring which was so complicated that no one could else understand it. And so accounting was born.

Words such as 'debits', 'credits', 'ledgers', 'day books', 'control accounts', 'accruals' and 'provisions' became an integral part of the accountant's language, the more cynical saying that this was in order to maintain the separation between those in the know from those outside, just as the same accusations have been levelled at computer 'technobuffs' in later years. The use of computers for accounting systems was, perhaps, one of the first steps in bringing the accountant's operation back within reach of other parts of the business and certainly today it would be normal to regard the data held within an accounting system as being an integral, and fundamental, part of the information structure of the whole organization.

Computerized accounting systems have been with us for a long time, indeed accounting was one of the first EDP (electronic data processing) tasks, back in the days when a computer could have usefully formed a backdrop in a science fiction movie, as opposed to today's quietly humming desktop, or even laptop, derivative. The history of accounting by computer is hence fairly well established, but that does not mean that the implementation of such systems necessarily runs smoothly. In the early days only the larger organizations had their own in-house computer systems, the remainder making do with bureau services or manual or mechanized ledger systems. Minicomputers and, more fundamentally, microcomputers, altered the accessibility of accounting software and many organizations took their first tentative steps in computing by tackling the accounting task.

The early days of computing now seem a long way away. In the 1990s the talk is of GUIs (graphical user interfaces), open systems, connectivity, structured query languages and, even in the microcomputer environment, powerful and robust multi-user and networked systems. Whereas the maintenance of ledgers was once a labour intensive task, conjuring up Dickensian images of straight-backed men with long coats sitting in strict silence on high stools with quill pens in their hands, it has progressively become so automated that even the initiation of many of the transactions is now driven by computer rather than by man. To paraphrase an old joke, given the increasing level of automation and integration with other systems, it is possible to imagine the computerized accounts system of the future being run by a man and a dog. The man will be there to feed the dog and the dog to bite the man if he looks as though he is going to touch anything.

While the human, rather than canine, influence predominates however, there will be a need to ensure that accounting systems are understood by those who use them and that they are introduced and run in an environment which is conducive to their success. It is these subjects which are to be tackled in this book and, no matter how advanced (or even simple) the system being introduced, the attention paid to the basic principles will be repaid many times over in the years (hopefully) of the system's successful running and expansion.

I have been involved in the introduction of a large number of accounting systems over the years, from the fairly large to the extremely small; from nationalized industries to one-man enterprises. Not all have been hugely successful but one consistent observation has been that, whatever the size of the organization, the chances of success are undoubtedly increased by responsible management of the exercise before, during and (just as importantly) after the introduction of the new system. In the final analysis, the performance of an accounting system, and the quality and timeliness of the information which is produced from it, are just as much reflections upon the manager responsible for it as the software itself. I have seen good accounting operations run from a base of software with limited facilities and, conversely, appalling messes generated when a 'high powered' package, full of bells and whistles, is in operation. The successful implementation of a system is not confined to buying a particular package and hoping everything else will work out and I hope that this book will ease the path of those who are treading what may be a somewhat unfamiliar route.

WHAT IS AN ACCOUNTING SYSTEM?

The term 'accounting system' can encapsulate many things and it is now appropriate to draw a border around the central theme of discussion in this book. An accounting system, for this purpose, is defined as the three ledgers, ie:

- sales ledger (also known as debtors ledger or accounts receivable);
- purchase ledger (also known as creditors ledger, bought ledger or accounts payable);
- nominal ledger (also known as general ledger).

The sales and purchase ledgers are often referred to as the 'personal' ledgers (as they relate to customers and suppliers, ie people) as opposed the named (hence 'nominal') accounts of the nominal ledger.

First, it must be recognized that, for many users, the above modules are often of secondary operational importance to those systems which frequently surround them, such as:

- sales order processing;
- sales invoicing;
- purchase order processing;
- stock control;
- bill of materials processing;
- job costing;
- fixed assets register;
- payroll.

All of the above impact in some way or another on an accounting system and will need to be input into the overall implementation and operational equation. A traditional form of diagram, showing the relationship between such modules in an integrated system is shown in Figure 1.1. In most cases, the use of such systems affect the timing, source and quality of transaction entry into the ledgers and comments made in this book about this subject will need to be read with this in mind. Whatever the scope of computerization, however, it is the accounting system which draws together all information of a financial nature and should provide the basis upon which all financial data within the organization is viewed.

All three ledgers are not always necessarily computerized or, if they are, are not always linked together. A small service based company having few customers and a low number of high value invoices may, for example, consider it worthwhile only computerizing the nominal ledger, whereas another, having a large number of customers and transactions but relatively few suppliers, may utilize sales and nominal ledgers but not acquire a purchase ledger. In larger organizations, an autonomous department may run a purchase ledger and, perhaps, a sales ledger locally, but the nominal ledger would be run centrally, possibly using different software and generically different hardware. In the majority of cases, however, all three ledgers are implemented as an integrated whole and it is this configuration from which the user is likely to gain most.

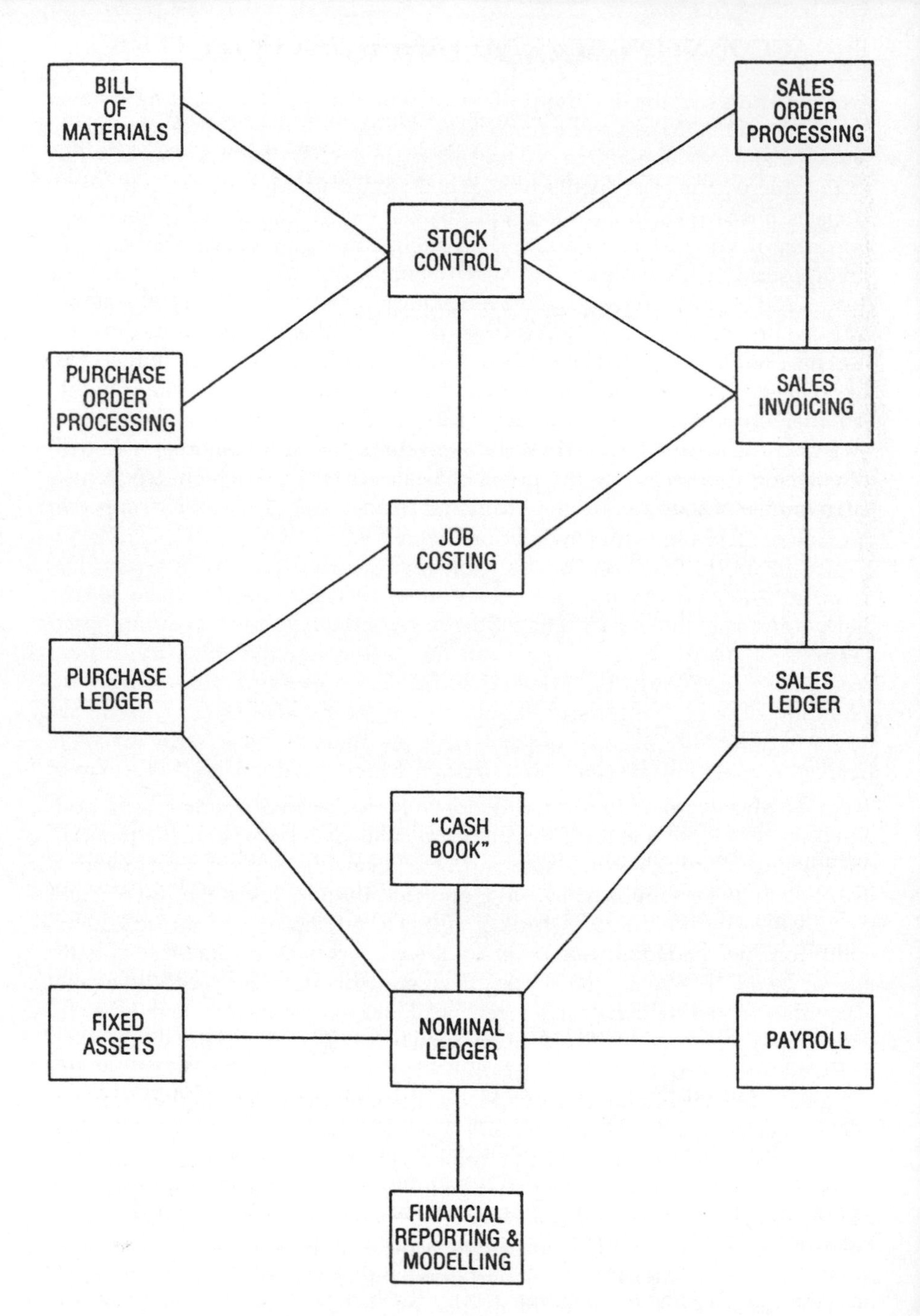

Figure 1.1 'Traditional' diagram showing typical relationships between modules of an integrated system

ACCOUNTING SYSTEMS ON MICROCOMPUTERS

The late 1970s saw the first influx of microcomputer based accounting systems in the UK and, although some reasonable products came to light, they quickly earned themselves something of a bad name, a taint which quickly spread also to the microcomputers themselves, at least in a business context. In some respects this was justified. Many early systems were designed for floppy, as opposed to hard, disk operation and, given the capacity constraints inherent in this approach (these were the days when a floppy drive could have a capacity as low as 100K), such systems had trouble in coping with any degree of volume. This led, for example, to a 'balance forward' method of operation for the sales and purchase ledgers in which all outstanding transactions were bundled into one balance figure for each customer and supplier by the end of period routine. Additionally, with just two low capacity floppy drives generally available to the system, not to mention a tiny (by today's standards) amount of memory, the task of effecting the update of the nominal ledger from the sales and purchase ledgers often called for considerable manual dexterity as disks were whipped in and out of the drives with bewildering frequency.

Not all the problems could be explained away by hardware constraints however. Some of the packages had obviously been developed in haste and/or naivety and bore the marks of this. Others were modified (or even unmodified) versions of American programs with the consequent difficulty, other than terminology, created by the British need for VAT accounting. Still others were painfully slow in operation, although, given the relative state of hardware technology, not all of this was necessarily attributable to the software. Most damaging of all, however, was that some packages contained little in the way of accounting controls, happily permitting, for example, single sided entries to be made to the ledgers. I still remember challenging one of the culprits at an exhibition stand in the early 1980s, only to be told: 'But some of our customers prefer it, they find double entry too confusing'. People who looked for an excuse to ridicule microcomputers in a business environment needed no better ammunition than this.

Times have changed of course, as has the perception of microcomputers, and modern accounting systems not only cope efficiently with large volumes, and with proper controls, but have also increasingly become involved with the more complex worlds of multi-company processing, multi-currency operation and interfaces with other systems – a far cry from the days of the dual floppy drive. In all of this time, thousands of managers have gained a first-hand experience of being at the sharp end of the installation of an accounting system and, it must be said, not every one has been an unremitting story of success. Some of the problems may have stemmed from 'bad luck' in the choice of hardware or software and others have their cause in the inexperience of the managers involved, either in computing or accounting terms, or frequently in both. The successful implementation of an accounting system requires a good understanding of the application itself, a thorough attention to detail and a sensible, and flexible, approach to planning. It is not something which can be done half-heartedly and, once implemented, the system will need to be continuously monitored to ensure that reliance can be placed on its results. While the same arguments can legitimately be put forward for any system, accounting systems are a case apart, a prime example of the strength and, at the same time, the vulnerability of computerized systems.

WHY ARE ACCOUNTING SYSTEMS DIFFERENT?

What is so special about accounting systems? After all, we have already noted that computers have been performing the task of accounting for many years and that there are many other business tasks which are more complex in computing terms than the mere shuffling of records which is grist to the accounting system's mill. While there is some truth in this, the decision to implement a computerized accounting system can never be taken lightly.

Few other systems are the subject of such scrutiny, both internally and externally (eg by external auditors), or governed by such rigidly defined and established rules and conventions. The accounting system becomes the central core of the business, the 'thermometer' by which the health of the business is assessed. If the thermometer is faulty, then the business may be heading for a long and possibly incurable illness. In order to perform the function well the accounting system must be kept reasonably up to date and must be properly controlled. There must be no question that the figures output from the system are anything other than concrete facts. While the same things may be said of other systems, committing your accounts to a computer means committing with a very large capital 'C'.

The use of computers for accounting systems has allowed, to some extent, for the 'de-skilling' of the accounting role or, to be more precise, of the traditional bookkeeping role. Through the use of accounting software it is possible for someone with little or no formal knowledge of accounting to run sales and purchase ledgers quite adequately (and many such people do). Even a nominal ledger, including the production of a (balanced) trial balance, can be run by inexperienced personnel, although this is an area where the knowledge might be wearing somewhat thin. For some, the *raison d'être* of a computerized accounting system is to be able to send decent looking statements out to customers and to provide some help with the VAT return. Fair enough, but it should still be recognized that the accounts which are eventually filed with the Registrar of Companies will be largely based upon the product of such a system. Also, incorrect information can lead to a failure to collect debts or to recognize impending liabilities and more than one company has been lulled into a false sense of security by a large debtors (and hence sales) figure being incorrectly shown by its computerized system. After all, it must be right, 'the computer says so'.

When people show such touching faith in their accounting systems it seems to be a hard fact of life that they are, from time to time, let down. Sometimes it is the fault of the hardware, sometimes the software and sometimes ... well, yes, sometimes even the user is to blame. Whatever happens, if something goes wrong with an accounting system you will be punished for it. Maybe not this month, maybe not next, but one day (at year-end perhaps?) you will hear the sound of someone saying: 'Ah yes, we did have a problem in January but we were too busy to look at it and we still managed to get our statements out so it didn't seem to matter too much.'

WHAT CAN GO WRONG?

Part of the battle is in being aware of what can go wrong; knowing the potential for disaster, however depressing that may be, at least equips one realistically for the task ahead. Looking at the world through the opposite of rose-tinted glasses, therefore, gives the following gloomy scenario.

Hardware problems

The bane of any system, hardware and related problems (such as power cuts) rarely mean good news for the intrepid accountant or bookkeeper. In fact, for 'rarely', read 'never'. If there is any processing of significance being performed when the problem is encountered you may have to go back to the drawing board, or at least to the last backup copy. A hardware problem may mean a bad area of disk in the middle of a file (eg your ledger) making the records contained in that sector unreadable. It may mean a file not being closed correctly, as may easily happen with an abnormal exit from a system, giving problems when accessed at a later stage. It may mean processing not being completed correctly, for example a ledger update adding only some of the intended transactions to the ledger.

Quite what you do about such events depends entirely on circumstance, the precise nature of the problem and what was being carried out at the time. In multi-user and networked systems it is necessary also to worry about the impact on other users, who may or may not have been affected by what has gone on at one point in the system. It is, however, more or less certain that you will have to do *something*. Some modern packages provide reasonable recovery routines which detect that a fault has occurred and may even be able to reconstruct the starting position so that the processing can be recommenced. Where the part of a disk holding a file has become unreadable, however, not even these will help and you will be left to reflect that your attempts to meet the month-end deadline for management accounts have fallen victim to the technological age. Hardware problems can befall the best of users, although the better the equipment is treated the better it tends to perform. By the same token, the worst disasters will normally befall the worst users, so it is very much in your own interests to try not to be one. Your insurance against such events is a controlled backup policy which is adhered to rigidly.

Software problems

The term 'software problems' covers a multitude of sins. If you have used a computer system, just think how many of the following charges you might have levelled at the software:

- □ badly written or designed;

- poor integration between modules;
- lack of flexibility;
- poor performance (ie slow);
- incomplete;
- lacking in controls;
- 'user unfriendly';
- fragile (ie not robust, keeps 'falling over');
- badly documented;
- unwieldy;
- poorly supported;
- lack of facilities;
- obsolete.

Sounds bleak, doesn't it? In fact not all of the above are likely to apply to any one system (you hope) and, to a certain extent, some of the problems can be overcome with a little resolution and fortitude if the end result is considered worthwhile.

There is, of course, no such entity as 'perfect' software. Even in the unlikely event of any software being absolutely bug free, it is improbable that the same software would appeal consistently to all users, irrespective of expertise, expectations, environment and requirements. Not only that, the software which might be 'perfect' today would become less so tomorrow as software fashions move ahead and users' requirements change. Many users do not find out the limitations of their software until they are up and running, or at least trying to reach that state, which is a bit late in the day as they may by then already be placing reliance on the system for day-to-day accounting operations.

Implementation problems

In many respects, the first hurdle of a computerized accounting system, ie its initial implementation, is one of the most difficult and this fence accounts for many fallers (or at least refusals) in the accounting systems steeplechase. The way in which the implementation of a new accounting system is planned, managed and executed will have a marked bearing upon its subsequent success or failure and, to continue with the racing analogy, those that struggle to clear this first hurdle can often find themselves falling into deep water on the other side.

By their nature, accounting systems do not operate in an isolated and controllable environment in which everything can stop while a new system gets going; even if you were willing or able to halt your own operations, suppliers will still send in invoices, customers will still pay you (you hope) and there will still be VAT and other statutory returns to make. Additionally, other than in a greenfield site, there will have been another accounting system, whether manual, machine driven or computerized, in operation and it will be necessary to effect a seamless and provable conversion from one to the other.

It is against this background that the new system must be taken on board and, to change sports, many users shoot themselves in the foot by making life more difficult than it need otherwise be.

Poor implementation can relate merely to the timing of the exercise, for example introducing a new system at the busiest time of the year for the accounts office is a fairly surefire method of getting things off to a bad start. This can be compounded by the choice of method of implementation; if it is decided, for example, to re-enter all transactions for the six months since the start of the current financial year and then run two systems in parallel for a further three months, you can hardly expect that nothing will buckle under the strain. A failure to explain new procedures and responsibilities to staff can damage their motivation and performance and hence that of the new system. Most, if not all, such problems can be avoided if a realistic implementation timetable is devised at the outset, allowing some contingency for things being less than perfect and ensuring that there is sufficient time for new procedures to be assimilated by those who are expected to practise them.

Operational problems

Once the initial implementation exercise is complete and the changeover from one system to another has been successfully concluded, it is still dangerous to start resting on your laurels as there are other factors which can prove just as troublesome at a later stage. An inappropriate hardware environment, for example, can disrupt an otherwise perfectly good system. This may be evidenced by having insufficient disk space available to run the application once the data volumes have built up to their 'live' level, slow printers which tie up the computer(s) and lack of memory which inhibits operation in a multi-user environment. None of these is likely to be insuperable, but it may be expensive or inconvenient to rectify them once the system is in full flow.

Operational problems are not necessarily just limited to the physical environment. The bane of many accounting systems, for example, is the poor coding conventions (for customers, suppliers, nominal codes, etc) which are in use. Once established, such conventions can be changed only with difficulty and the hapless users are often left to struggle with meaningless account codes which do little to help identify the records to which they relate. Even trivial sounding matters such as filing assume importance when they go wrong and if all the time were handed back to those who had whiled away hours looking for invoices which had 'gone missing' then they would probably be able to look forward to a few more years after retirement!

Management problems

Many problems in the world of computerized accounting systems derive from a lack of understanding by management of some of the golden rules for implementation and operation. For example, inadequate forethought applied to staff resources and training can be a fundamental barrier to success and staff also need to be made conscious of their revised responsibilities, particularly those which are computer-specific such as taking backup copies and batch operation, under the new regime. Management can also help by scheduling the major tasks, such as disk intensive ledger updates or lengthy reports, so that staff are not held up unnecessarily by other users of the system.

It is, however, in the area of controls where management will have the most important role to play and there must be a recognition that controls will need to apply around the system as well as within it. There will always be those who will tend to say 'well, if the computer says so it must be right', but this can never be a more dangerous assumption (if misplaced, that is) than in an accounting system. Implementation of control procedures is not sufficient in itself, they must also be enforced and reviewed by management as part of a routine periodic task. This need not be a time-consuming exercise, particularly if the system is run tidily and efficiently, but rarely will time be better spent.

With all this potential to go wrong, why does anyone bother? The answer, of course, is that not only is there much to be gained from computerizing the accounting function but that, in many cases, it would not be possible to survive, let alone grow in terms of trading volumes, without doing so. While it is as well to be aware of what can go wrong, and many of these themes will be returned to later in the book, it is only fair to end on a more positive note and to look at some of the benefits which can be expected.

What can go right?

The advantages of computerizing the accounts and related functions should really extend far wider than the automated production of financial accounts, although that is, of course, a good place to start listing advantages. The mentality adopted by some in which the newly computerized process is merely replacing a manual system or an existing computerized system which is now obsolete invariably leads to under-utilization of the new system and the unthinking continuation of practices which may have had their foundation in another era.

Any list of benefits can hardly pretend to be exhaustive and, of course, not all benefits may be available from all systems although this may be just as much a dysfunction of management as a criticism of the software employed. It is, however, worth looking at some of the advantages which would normally be gained by computerizing the ledger functions.

- The proper rules of double entry bookkeeping should be automatically applied, ie debits will actually be equal to credits!
- Because of this, a trial balance produced from the nominal ledger should always be in balance. (Note that it may not necessarily be correct, this naturally depends upon the transactions entered by the user, but the tedious task of getting a trial balance to balance should be removed.)
- There will, by definition, be some consistency in the recording of information for each transaction entered to the system.
- Automatic numbering sequences can be applied and controlled where relevant, eg in the numbering of transaction input batches and nominal ledger journals.
- Validation of critical items of data will be applied at the point of entry of transactions or master file records.
- There will be a base of customer (and supplier) records which may be useful in terms of marketing information and action.

- Within each ledger, there is only one point of entry of a transaction to the system, ie there is no necessity to transcribe a transaction from one accounting record (eg a day book) to another (eg a ledger) as there is in a manual system.
- There will be an automatic interface between the personal ledgers (ie sales and purchase) and the nominal ledger, again removing the need for any duplication of input for any transaction and hence removing the opportunity for the introduction of errors.
- In the sales and purchase ledgers the allocation (ie matching) of cash receipts and payments to the invoices to which they relate will be both simplified and subsequently clearly defined.
- On-screen enquiry facilities enhance the impression of immediate accessibility of accounting information. Similarly, the production of reports 'at the touch of a button' helps users to manage the system and to feel in control of events.
- A computerized system is likely to lend itself to the provision of information for the compilation of VAT information required on returns for Customs & Excise.
- The discipline enforced by the use of a computer system tends to facilitate the operation of control procedures and the production of evidence that they have been applied.
- The basic operations of transaction entry may be carried out by personnel who do not necessarily have formal bookkeeping training.
- Possibilities exist for interface and even interaction of information with other systems. This can be the transfer of data between other software modules (eg sales invoicing or purchase order processing), with remote systems, with other types of application (eg the transfer of information to and from spreadsheets) and even with such 'non-accounting' applications as word processing (WP) (eg for the production of letters to debtors) and desktop publishing (DTP) systems for a professional presentation of information.
- The production of information through the analysis of data entered is of paramount importance. A universal example of this is the ageing analysis of debtors or creditors, a task which would be at the least difficult in a manual system. Indeed, there is virtually a limitless scope of information which can be gleaned from an accounting system by imaginative managers.
- The use of cost centres in a nominal ledger enables transactions to be analysed additionally by operational division or any other convenient entity without unnecessarily complicating the nominal coding structure defined for financial reporting.
- Credit and cash control disciplines in respect of both customers and suppliers can be immeasurably sharpened by having better and more up-to-date information easily to hand. The ability to produce, for example, timely and accurate customer statements can help to improve the collection of debts or at least accelerate the resolution of queries.
- Facilities such as automatic reversal of accruals and prepayments, standard (ie recurring) journals, budgetary control fields and report writing modules greatly simplify not only the production of timely and

meaningful accounts but also their presentation in an attractive and professional manner.

- Not only should a computerized system permit the accommodation of present trading levels within its routine operation, it should also allow for their expansion. This ability to cope easily with a growth in transaction volumes without the need for a similar impact on staffing levels is fundamental to the acceptance of many accounting systems.
- The preparation of records and presentation of accounts for audit purposes is likely to be less disruptive and, particularly with the more popular accounting software packages, the audit firm may well have some familiarity with its operation, thus saving further time and costs.

The above factors are likely to form too powerful an argument in all but the smallest of businesses and, particularly with the rapid growth in the use of business microcomputers in the 1980s, it is now becoming increasingly rare to find an established organization which is 'going on to the computer' for the first time. Whatever the underlying motivation may be, however, remember that, above all, a computerized accounting system should enable proper accounting records to be easily maintained; if a system cannot do this, no matter what else it may be capable of, it is not worth the space on your computer's disk.

In the following chapters we look at some of the secrets for the successful implementation of a computerized accounting system. Some of these factors would apply for any system but, given the 'real time' nature of the accounting operation, in which the world moves on remorselessly each day in terms of accounting transactions, there can be little margin for error and, having embarked on an incorrect course, it can be very difficult subsequently to change direction.

2

Basic Principles of Accounting

ARE DEBITS STILL NEAREST THE WINDOW?

This chapter and the next set out basic principles in two respects. First, in gaining an understanding of the principles of accounting which may benefit those without an accounting training or even those with one who are in need of a refresher. Secondly, in Chapter 3, adapting those principles into an understanding of how a computerized accounting system actually works. For this part of the exercise a hypothetical system is used and while this is not intended to reflect any particular software package, the underlying principles of processing which are described are sound and would result in a working system.

Is it really necessary to understand both the accounting and computing aspects? Certainly if you already have a good understanding of accounting and, for that matter, of computerized accounting, you can probably skip quite happily on to the next chapter. Alternatively you may neither know nor care about the foundations upon which an accounting system is built, as long as it does the job for you as and when required and it keeps your auditors happy. Fair enough, but such a reliance may add to the pressure at some stage in the future when something goes amiss and you are flying blind as to the cause of the problem and, more importantly, what needs to be done about it.

As anyone who has worked in an accounts office knows, there is an old tongue-in-cheek saying that 'debits go nearest the window', and while this might have led to a large scale reshuffling of the furniture in some organizations it was probably comforting to know that there was at least some point of the compass from which to take reference as clerks laboured with their manuscript schedules and bound ledger volumes. The introduction of computers has doubtless been both good and bad news for people in need of such orientation. In Chapter 1 we noted the argument that the use of a computer has 'de-skilled' the bookkeeping task, that as long as the operator picks the correct mode of entry for a transaction and is accurate in other respects so that, for example, the amount is entered correctly and to the correct account, then the computer will automatically post the input in accordance with the rules of accounting. This is, of course, absolutely true (except in the case of journal input into any of the ledgers) and I have certainly yet to come across a computer which takes the window, or any other part of the office, as its reference point! This view does, however, ignore the experience required to know what to do when something goes wrong and, for that matter, to recognize when something has gone wrong. Users who plough merrily on with a trial balance which is out of balance or with the debtors or creditors control accounts in disagreement with the personal ledgers to which they relate are likely to get themselves deeper and deeper into trouble and the time and cost of getting out of it may increase almost exponentially as each accounting period goes by.

Before continuing, it is worth emphasizing that, in drawing comparisons between manual and computerized methods of maintaining accounting records, it is only the methods which are different and not the underlying principles of accounting involved. Hence, computerized accounting is not some special form of accounting with its own rules and regulations, but rather a different method of doing the same job, albeit with the potential to achieve far more, particularly in the area of related management information, than could ever be contemplated without the use of a computer.

THE ACCOUNTING PART

Books of prime entry

There are possibly more books available to explain the principles of accounting than any other subject, so there is little point in devoting numerous pages of text to it in this volume. Such is the 'user friendliness' of many software packages that it is just about possible to run an accounting system without any real knowledge of accounting (and some users, particularly those in smaller companies, do) but, inevitably, some understanding of what is really going on radically increases the potential of the system.

For those who feel a barrier in this area some reminders of the main elements involved in accounting may not go amiss, although a more formal and detailed text would be recommended for those who wish to delve more deeply. Lapsing into accounting jargon for a moment, there are certain records in which transactions are first recorded in a formal accounting fashion when they are raised or received by an organization. Not surprisingly these records are called books of prime entry and include the following.

Sales day book

This records, in chronological order, sales invoices (and credit notes) which have been raised. The details shown will include the invoice date, number, customer name, gross value, VAT amount and the net amount split among a number of columns showing the type of sale which has been made. This latter element effectively reflects the analysis required for posting the transaction to the nominal ledger.

Purchase day book

Similar in concept to the sales day book, this is used to record purchase invoices (and credit notes) received from suppliers. Again the split of the net amount of each invoice, in terms of defining the type of expenditure incurred, will determine the form in which the invoice is recorded in the nominal ledger.

Cash book

The volume in which the receipt and issue of cheques and other transactions relating to the bank account(s) are recorded is the cash book. Traditionally, one side of the cash book is used for receipts (with sub-totals of amounts actually banked to facilitate subsequent reconciliation with the bank statement) and the other, usually with more room for analysis, for payments made from the bank account including cheques, standing orders and bank charges and interest.

Petty cash book

Petty cash refers to the ready cash used for incidental office expenses and this is recorded in a similar fashion to bank account movements in the cash book.

The journal

The journal is the volume in which transactions not covered by any of the other books of prime entry are recorded. A typical journal, for example, would be in respect of the accounting entries made in respect of depreciation of fixed assets.

The ledgers

Transactions are recorded in the books of prime entry in chronological order, ie as they occur, and while this is fundamental in tracing the trail of a transaction from its source, it is not very helpful in terms of assessing or controlling events which relate to particular accounts. For this reason, transactions are transcribed (or posted) to a ledger in which they are grouped by account and this is where the feared terms 'debit' and 'credit' arise. One of the fundamental concepts of accounting is that the sum of amounts which are recorded as debits must be equal to those recorded as credits. By convention, debits are used to show:

- assets (eg fixed assets such as fixtures and fittings and motor cars or current assets such as stock, debtors or funds in a bank account);
- expenses (eg purchases, accommodation and payroll costs);
- losses (from trading or profit and loss accounts);

and credits to show:

- liabilities (eg bank loans, overdrafts, trade creditors and other creditors such as those in respect of PAYE and VAT);
- income (eg from sales);
- profits (from trading or profit and loss accounts);
- equity (ie share capital – the funding of the business).

The balance on any particular account (from whatever ledger) is found by taking the difference between the total values of the debit and credit entries; if the debits are greater than the credits then the account is said to have a debit balance and if the credits are greater then it has a credit balance. A simple example of a bank account can be used to illustrate this:

DEBITS		CREDITS	
Balance brought fwd	2,000	Cheque to B	300
Received from A	100	Bank charges	50
Received from C	200	Cheque to D	100
Received from E	300		

The balance on the account is £2,600 (total debits) minus £450 (total credits), which therefore results in a debit balance of £2,150. Note that cheques received *debit* the bank account and cheques paid out *credit* it. This often confuses those who are new to the concepts, particularly as it does not accord with the bank statements received by customers, but it can be explained quite simply in terms of the accounting conventions already established. This is because bank statements are extracts from *their* (ie the banks') books of account and, to the banks, the money you deposit represents a liability (and therefore a credit) in terms of their relationship with you because they effectively owe this money to you. In *your* books, however, the money received is most definitely an asset (ie cash in your bank) and hence this results in a debit to the bank (or cash book control) account maintained in your accounting records.

In concept there need only be one ledger (a nominal ledger) but, for ease of handling, principal subdivisions of this are often dealt with as separate entities, the link between these sub- ledgers and the main ledger being monitored by the use of control accounts which reflect the overall balance of the sub-ledgers within the main ledger. Two such sub-ledgers are the sales ledger, which is used to control debtors (ie customers who owe money) and the purchase ledger, which is used to control creditors (ie suppliers to whom money is owed) and, as noted in Chapter 1, these are sometimes referred to as the personal ledgers. While it would be perfectly possible to hold all customer and supplier accounts as individual accounts within the nominal ledger this would normally be unwieldy and would obscure the functionality of that ledger. The use of these three ledgers can be summarized as follows.

Sales ledger

This is the accounting record used to control debtors, ie customers who owe you money. Sales invoices raised debit (because debtors are assets) the customer accounts in the sales ledger and credits are formed by cash receipts, credit notes and discounts allowed. The balance on any one account is the amount owed by that customer and the total of all the individual customer balances should be reflected as the trade debtors figure in the nominal ledger.

Purchase ledger

This is the accounting record used to control creditors, ie suppliers to whom you owe money. Purchase invoices received credit (because creditors are liabilities) the supplier accounts in the purchase ledger and debits are formed by cash payments, credit notes and discounts received. The balance on any one account is the amount owed to that supplier and the total of all the individual supplier balances should be reflected as the trade creditors figure in the nominal ledger.

Nominal ledger

The nominal ledger is the principal ledger and the one from which the trial balance is produced in addition to management reports such as the profit and loss account and balance sheet. The trial balance is effectively a list of balances of all the accounts maintained on the nominal ledger and remember that this will include the control accounts which govern the sales and purchase ledgers. By definition, a trial balance should show that the total of debit and credit balances is equal.

Control accounts

Mention has been made of control accounts and an understanding of their operation is important. The concept that the personal ledgers (ie the sales and purchase ledgers) are merely convenient subdivisions of the main (ie nominal) ledger has already been introduced. If such a subdivision is made however (and it very nearly always is in a computerized system) then it becomes paramount that the total of the balances in each of the personal ledgers is accurately reflected in the nominal. The mechanism of such a reconciliation is effected through the use of control accounts.

The nominal ledger will contain two accounts, usually called something like debtors control and creditors control, which represent the total of all the balances on the sales and purchase ledgers respectively. Postings are made to these accounts in summary (eg the total of a batch of invoices may form one entry on this account) so that the movement on these accounts is normally easy to review and to check against the ledger from which they derive. In a manual accounting system, for example, postings would be made to the control accounts from the totals of the day books and cash book for that period, the individual transactions being posted in detail to the constituent accounts within the source ledger.

In a computerized or mechanized accounting system a control account is often also maintained within each of the personal ledgers as, apart from aiding review against the equivalent nominal ledger postings, it also facilitates the internal checking that the transaction files are in balance. If, say, a batch of sales invoices totalled £3,450, the following entries may be made by the system:

- SALES LEDGER
  Debit the individual customer accounts with the invoices totalling £3,450.
  Credit the control account record maintained in the sales ledger with the total of the batch, ie with £3,450.
- NOMINAL LEDGER
  Credit the VAT account and the individual sales nominal codes with the

analysis of the invoices totalling £3,450.
Debit the debtors control account with £3,450.
From the above it can easily be seen that:
(a) the debit and credit entries balance within each ledger;
(b) the balance on the debtors control account in the nominal ledger (ie £3,450 debit) reflects the total of the individual customer balances in the sales ledger;
(c) the balance on the control account record in the sales ledger (ie £3,450 credit) is equal and opposite to that on the debtors control account in the nominal ledger.

To take the example further, if a batch of cash receipts were then entered, total value being £2,500, then:

- SALES LEDGER
  Credit the individual customer accounts with the receipts totalling £2,500.
  Debit the control account record maintained in the sales ledger with the total of the batch, ie with £2,500.
- NOMINAL LEDGER
  Debit the bank account with £2,500.
  Credit the debtors control account with £2,500.

Assuming no brought forward value, the balance on the debtors control account would then be £950, which accurately represents the sum of the individual customer accounts in the sales ledger.

The processing of purchase ledger transactions follows a similar course except that the balance of the control record in the purchase ledger would normally be debit (because the individual purchase invoices are recorded as credits) and the creditors control account in the nominal ledger would thus normally show a credit balance.

Transaction types

Having got this far, it is now worth summarizing the accounting effect of the common transaction types encountered in an accounting system.

- SALES LEDGER

Effect on sales ledger	*Effect on nominal ledger*
Invoice	
Debit customer account	Credit VAT and sales accounts
Credit control record	Debit debtors control
Credit note	
Credit customer account	Debit VAT and sales accounts
Debit control record	Credit debtors control
Cash receipt	
Credit customer account	Debit bank
Debit control record	Credit debtors control

Cash discount allowed	
Credit customer account	Debit discounts allowed
Debit control record	Credit debtors control
Adjustment	
Debit/credit customer	Debit/credit nominated account
Credit/debit control	Credit/debit debtors control

□ PURCHASE LEDGER

Effect on purchase ledger	*Effect on nominal ledger*
Invoice	
Credit supplier account	Debit VAT and purchase/ expenditure accounts
Debit control record	Credit creditors control
Credit note	
Debit supplier account	Credit VAT and purchase/ expenditure accounts
Credit control record	Debit creditors control
Cash payment	
Debit supplier account	Credit bank
Credit control record	Debit creditors control
Cash discount received	
Debit supplier account	Credit discounts received
Credit control record	Debit creditors control
Adjustment	
Credit/debit supplier	Debit/credit nominated account
Debit/credit control	Credit/debit creditors control

□ NOMINAL LEDGER

Journal	Debit/credit nominated account(s) Credit/debit nominated account(s)
Cash book payments	Debit nominated expenditure accounts Credit bank
Cash book receipts	Credit nominated income accounts Debit bank

Armed with this knowledge, we can now go on to see how a specimen computer system handles these transactions.

3

Accounting by Computer

ACCOUNTING BY COMPUTER

Despite the obvious similarity of ledger systems there are many different methods used by software companies for the structure and relationship of the various data files which comprise a working system. Nevertheless, there is normally a common link which can be distilled and directly related to the manual counterpart. The following paragraphs assume a fairly elementary set of principal files but they are sufficient to form the basis of a working computerized accounting system. They should, however, be read in the context that they do not describe how any one system works, but rather the conceptual sequence of events; a live system would undoubtedly demonstrate more sophistication and complexity.

One difference which is worth noting, however, is the point in a computerized system at which an accounting entry can be considered to have been made, particularly as this is something which often perplexes less experienced users. To set matters straight, a transaction can only be considered to be a true accounting entry if it is not subsequently possible to amend or delete it in any way other than through the further input of other valid transactions to the same ledger as, for example, when a credit note is used to cancel an invoice which is raised in error. This problem applies particularly to accounting systems as the process of transaction input frequently involves the entries initially residing 'in limbo' on some sort of batch file which is available for direct editing, or even deletion, before it is posted to the ledger. In such circumstances, the use of, for example, a batch entry report as an 'accounting record' (sometimes in the mistaken belief that it forms an acceptable alternative to a day book report), ie as proof of input to the ledger, would be incorrect, as any transactions contained thereon could subsequently have been amended or deleted (or further transactions added) and hence the report may not reflect the actual state of the ledger. Only reports which are produced *after* the point of accounting entry can therefore be regarded as true accounting documents.

Are debits positive or negative?

The joke about debits being nearest the window in a manual system prompts the question as to how the orientation of a transaction (or, indeed, a balance) is held within a computer file. In essence, one (or a combination of) the following methods are likely to be used in any one system.

1. Each monetary value is held with a positive or negative sign. This would normally be used to denote that debits are positive and credits negative, *except* in the purchase ledger where the reverse may be true, thus enabling invoices to be shown as positive amounts.
2. Separate fields are used to hold debit and credit amounts, which are thus always recorded as positive figures. While there are some advantages with such an approach it is likely to be wasteful of space where fixed length records are in use.
3. The amounts are always recorded as positive, a separate indicator field being used to denote whether the value should be construed as debit or credit.

The means by which this is effected should have no impact on the user, who should normally see transactions displayed or printed as positive figures where the context is obvious. In the examples covered in the rest of this chapter, option (1) is used.

Allocations

An important area of difference between a computerized and manual accounting system is the concept of allocations. 'Allocation' is the term used to denote the matching of:

- on the sales ledger, cash receipts (and credit notes) against outstanding sales invoices to which they relate;
- on the purchase ledger, cash payments (and credit notes) against outstanding purchase invoices to which they relate.

As an illustration, say a sales ledger account (with account code AAR001) contained the following transactions:

ACCOUNT	TYPE	VALUE
AAR001	INV	235.00
AAR001	INV	1,000.00
AAR001	CRN	–30.00
AAR001	INV	470.00
AAR001	INV	235.00
Balance on account =		£1,910.00

If, say, a cheque for £1,675 was received from AAR001, this would be added to the ledger as follows:

ACCOUNT	TYPE	VALUE
AAR001	INV	235.00
AAR001	INV	1,000.00
AAR001	CRN	–30.00
AAR001	INV	470.00
AAR001	INV	235.00
AAR001	REC	–1,675.00
Balance on account =		£235.00

In terms of the account entries required this would be sufficient for the recording of the transactions but, in a computerized system in particular, there is the necessity of identifying those transactions to which the receipt relates and of somehow flagging those transactions as having been 'allocated' against each other. This serves two purposes:

1. during the course of the period, the balance of the account can be more clearly seen by looking only at those transactions which are unallocated (or which are partly allocated, a concept we shall come to shortly);
2. at period end, the ledger can be purged of those transactions which have been fully allocated, leaving only those which are unallocated (or partly allocated) to be carried forward into the next period. This is the basis of an 'open item' accounting system, contrasting with a 'balance forward' method of approach in which all outstanding transactions are consolidated into one figure at period end for each account.

Depending upon the system, the allocation process may be carried out by the user during the entry of cash or credit note transactions, outstanding transactions being presented on screen for flagging as required, or, in more sophisticated systems, some form of automatic allocation may be attempted in which the amount entered is allocated against outstanding transactions in chronological order, a process which is likely to work successfully in the majority of cases. In the example used, the account may look like this after allocation:

ACCOUNT	TYPE	VALUE	ALLOC (X = allocated)
AAR001	INV	235.00	X
AAR001	INV	1,000.00	X
AAR001	CRN	–30.00	X
AAR001	INV	470.00	X
AAR001	INV	235.00	
AAR001	REC	–1,675.00	X
Balance on account =		£235.00	

Note that the balance of the account is unaffected by the allocation process and that the transactions themselves are unaltered in any way other than by the setting of an allocation flag. Note also that allocation permits the receipt to be allocated against specific transactions; the above example could equally have shown the second invoice for £235.00 as having been allocated instead of the first if, for example, the first invoice was in dispute or had been overlooked by the customer.

The concept of partial allocation has also been mentioned. This is not permitted by all systems but, as the name implies, it relates to instances where only part of a transaction is marked as having been cleared. To return to the example, supposing the receipt had been for £1,600 instead of £1,675. This might have been allocated as:

ACCOUNT	TYPE	VALUE	O/S VALUE
AAR001	INV	235.00	0.00
AAR001	INV	1,000.00	0.00
AAR001	CRN	–30.00	0.00
AAR001	INV	470.00	75.00
AAR001	INV	235.00	235.00
AAR001	REC	–1,600.00	0.00
Balance on account =		£310.00	£310.00

It is immediately obvious that such an approach requires a different basis of processing, ie to record the outstanding amount after allocation as well as the original value of the transaction. Some argue against the use of partial allocations, saying that they make for untidy ledgers and certainly it is often better to avoid them (leaving transactions unallocated until a complete and fully allocatable set of transactions is on the ledger) but, particularly in certain industries where payments on account are common, they may be unavoidable.

A set of accounting files

Not surprisingly, most computerized ledger systems will have data files which reflect, to some extent, the books of prime entry and ledgers referred to in the first part of this chapter. Hence, there would normally be a specific data file which would be identifiable as, say, the nominal ledger and another from which the day book type of reports would be produced. A computerized system is, however, much more than merely an electronic replication of manual methods and, in addition to these transaction files, there will be other data files which are fundamental to the operation of the system. These include the following.

Master files

These are files used for recording standing details and other information relating to customers (for a sales ledger), suppliers (purchase ledger) and nominal codes and cost centres (nominal ledger).

Reference files

These contain system constants, such as VAT rates or user generated report definitions, for example those required for profit and loss or balance sheet prints.

Input files

These are holding files used for the initial input of transactions to the system pending their confirmation as accounting entries.

Analysis files

Analysis files are those required for, say, VAT reporting or sales by product by customer matrix reporting in systems which are linked to invoicing and stock modules.

Index files

These are internal files used by a system to enable the rapid look up of data by reference to specified key fields, such as the customer account number on a sales ledger file.

Work files

Work files are more internal files which may be generated by a system during certain operations, for example during a purchase ledger automated payments run, or for the purposes of producing a specific report.

With the above in mind, it is worth looking at the structure and operation of a hypothetical system. 'Hypothetical' is very much the operative word, as actual systems will vary in many ways and it is the principles of processing which are being illustrated here, rather than the detail of any one system.

Suppose that our hypothetical system contained the following principal data files:

- **Input files**
  SBF : sales batch invoice/credit input file
  PBF : purchase batch invoice/credit input file
  SCF : sales cash input file
  PCF : purchase cash input file
  NBF : nominal journal batch input file

- **Ledger and day book files**
  SLF : sales ledger file
  PLF : purchase ledger file
  NLF : nominal ledger file
  NPF : nominal postings file
  DBF : day book file(s)

- **Analysis file**
  VRF : VAT report file

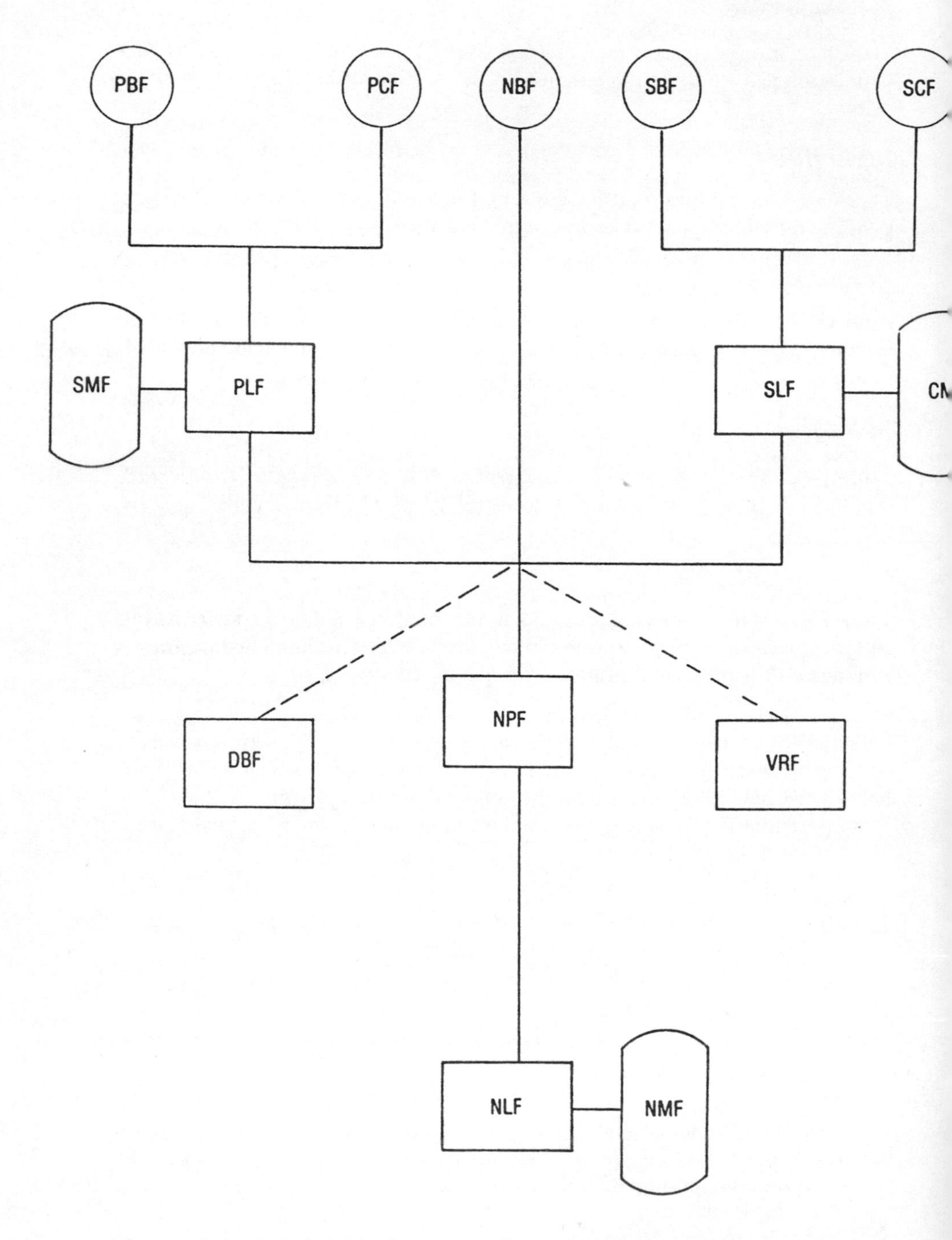

Figure 3.1 Relationship between principal data files in our hypothetical system

- **Master files**
  CMF : customer master file
  SMF : supplier master file
  NMF : nominal master file

The relationship of the files is shown in Figure 3.1 and the functions and outline structures of the individual files are described in the paragraphs which follow. As we have already noted, in addition to the above, any real system would be likely to have a further set of data files, for example to store changeable parameters such as period numbers and the format in which nominal ledger management reports are to be printed. Such files are, however, peripheral to the principal path of operation of the system and are hence excluded from our simplified example.

Sales batch invoice/credit input file (SBF)

One record per sales ledger transaction plus further records for nominal ledger analysis.

This is an initial input file upon which batches of sales ledger transactions are held before being passed to the sales ledger by a subsequent posting routine. These transactions will include invoices (including any passed automatically from a linked invoicing and order processing system), credit notes, adjustments and, depending upon the processing methods employed, cash receipts.

Transactions on this file which have been entered directly to the sales ledger may not yet form accounting entries as they may be added to, amended or deleted (or a whole batch may even be deleted) before a sales ledger update is effected.

The type of data contained on such a file would include:

- customer account number;
- transaction reference;
- transaction type;
- transaction date;
- batch number;
- period number;
- gross value;
- VAT value;
- nominal analysis of net value (depending upon the method of processing, this may entail further records being contained on the file, eg one additional record for each separate nominal code);
- VAT analysis of net value (ie zero rate, standard rate, etc);
- remarks.

Note that this or any other transaction file would be unlikely to include the name of the customer as this lengthy descriptive item would invariably be looked up on the customer master file (CMF), using the account number as the index key, as and when it is required during processing.

Sales cash input file (SCF)

One record per cash receipt.

Depending upon the type of processing involved, sales ledger cash receipts may use the same input files as invoice and credit note transactions, in which case no separate file for cash entries would exist. Cash does however have different processing requirements and, in particular, must interact with the sales ledger itself so that allocation against outstanding invoices can be easily effected. Other dissimilarities between cash and invoice/credit note processing are that the former is unlikely to have multiple nominal analysis requirements (the nominal analysis being normally either to a defined bank account or to discounts allowed) and there is also no need for any recording in respect of VAT. These dissimilarities are often sufficient to persuade system designers to adopt different processing methods from those for invoices and credit notes and hence to define input files with different structures.

Sales ledger file (SLF)

One record per sales ledger transaction.

This is the ledger itself; transactions will be passed from the batch input file and the cash input file and added to this when a ledger update (or posting) is effected. Transactions on this file are, by definition, accounting entries and it should not be possible directly to amend them in any way; the only method of amendment should be through the use of further transactions which will automatically preserve the 'trail' of the sequence of processing events.

A typical sales ledger record would include:

- ☐ customer account number;
- ☐ transaction date;
- ☐ transaction type;
- ☐ transaction number;
- ☐ batch number;
- ☐ period number;
- ☐ gross value;
- ☐ VAT value (possibly, but not necessarily);
- ☐ remarks.

The sales ledger file also contains a set of records relating to a control account so that the integrity of the file can be easily checked by ensuring that it balances to zero.

Customer master file (CMF)

One record per customer.

The file on which customer contact and analysis details are maintained in addition to various other items of balance related information. One record may be used as a sales ledger control account record. If the system was one which permitted multiple delivery addresses for a linked order processing module, then further subsidiary records may be held for each customer for these as may also be the case if separate statement addresses were permitted.

A typical customer record would include:

- account number;
- customer name;
- address (say four or five lines);
- telephone, telex, fax and other contact details;
- current balance;
- turnover figures for current and previous years;
- credit details (for use by order processing and invoicing modules);
- various indicators for analysis of customer, eg representative code, area code, customer type.

Purchase ledger files

The equivalent files for the purchase ledger would be similar to those of the sales ledger and some systems may even physically use the same files, distinguishing between purchase and sales transactions by means of internal indicators. One important difference, however, is that most computerized purchase ledgers show credit items as positive (so that purchase invoices can be shown as positive rather than negative) and, depending upon the means of internal representation used, this may have repercussions for the way in which transactions are passed to the nominal posting file (NPF).

Effectively, much of purchase ledger processing is a replica of that used in a sales ledger (and vice versa) and it is not uncommon, therefore, for software companies to base the development of one ledger upon the code which has already been written for the other. This not only has the advantage in terms of time saved by the developers (and, ultimately, costs saved by the user), but also helps the uniformity of appearance and consistency between the two ledgers.

Nominal journal batch input file (NBF)

This file would be used to hold journals input direct to the nominal ledger and other related types of transactions such as cash book or petty cash input. Transactions would be passed to the nominal postings file when the journals are confirmed as completed for inclusion in the next nominal ledger update.

Nominal postings file (NPF)

This intermediate file between the sales/purchase ledgers and the nominal ledger will contain details of transactions which have been posted to the personal ledgers and also those entered through the nominal journal input stream. All of these transactions would next require posting to the nominal ledger. By definition, the debit entries on such a file must be equal to the credits, but the degree of summarization of transactions for posting to the nominal ledger may differ between packages. Some of the options on the spectrum of summarization are as follows.

- Each individual line of nominal analysis for each personal ledger transaction can be posted to the nominal ledger as a discrete transaction.

This can result in a large nominal ledger file, particularly if sales invoice data is received with multiple line entries for the same nominal code within the same invoice.

- Summarization can be effected by individual transaction (ie no more than one record for any one nominal code for any single transaction).
- Summarization can be effected by a batch of transactions (ie only one record for each nominal code included in a batch of transactions).
- Summarization can be effected by run of the postings routine (which may comprise a number of batches).

Hence, the actual content of such a file will vary according to the processing philosophy adopted and, just as importantly, the report which is to be produced at the time of the nominal ledger update.

Nominal master file (NMF)

The nominal master file is used to record details of nominal codes and cost centres and will be used for recording the descriptions and characteristics (eg whether profit and loss or balance sheet item) as well as for validation of nominal codes and cost centres entered at any point in the system. Depending upon the processing philosophy, this file may also hold budget and period end balance details, but these are sometimes recorded in a separate file.

Typical fields would include:

- nominal code;
- description;
- type of account (eg profit and loss or balance sheet);
- current balance;
- previous period balances (possibly);
- previous year balances (possibly);
- budgets (possibly).

The nominal master file may also be used to record details of cost centres or departments which are in use by the system.

Nominal ledger file (NLF)

Then there is the nominal ledger itself; this file will contain one record for each nominal ledger transaction and is the ultimate destination for all transactions processed by the system. Typical fields would be:

- nominal code;
- cost centre or department code;
- transaction date;
- transaction type;
- transaction reference;
- transaction source (eg sales, purchase or nominal);
- period to which it relates;
- period in which it was entered;

- value, plus some form of indicator to determine whether debit or credit, eg this may take the form of a minus sign to denote a credit item;
- remarks.

Note that the records would be unlikely to include a description of the nominal code or cost centre as this would be looked up interactively from the NMF during processing.

Day book file (DBF)

This file will be needed to hold details of purchase and sales invoices, credit notes and adjustments in sufficient detail to produce day book reports at the end of the accounting period. Hence it will need to record at least:

- account number;
- transaction reference;
- transaction date;
- transaction type;
- gross value;
- VAT value;
- nominal analysis of net value.

In practice, one of the other system files may be used for this purpose, perhaps the batch input file or the nominal postings file and, of course, separate files may be used for sales and purchase ledger items, although this would not necessarily be the case providing that the entries on the file were suitably flagged.

VAT report file (VRF)

The VAT report file would be required to provide the supporting detail for the quarterly return made to Customs & Excise, detailing the VAT related transactions during the quarter and the various rates of VAT applying to them. Again, the requirement could conceivably be satisfied by expanding the use of another file, but remember that the detail needs to be held for VAT purposes in three-monthly blocks which has implications for the frequency with which any combined file could be cleared down and space recovered.

A typical set of data fields would be:

- account number;
- transaction reference;
- transaction date;
- transaction type;
- gross value;
- VAT value (total);
- VAT analysis of net value by VAT rate.

A WORKED EXAMPLE

To set matters in perspective it would be useful to work through a simple example which illustrates the main processing stream of a system based on the types of files described above. To keep matters as straightforward as possible, we shall look at a couple of sales invoices and a cash receipt from a customer; the principles from this snapshot can then be easily extended to other transaction types.

For the purposes of this exercise a skeleton set of nominal codes can be assumed, eg:

101 : sales of product A
102 : sales of product B
801 : cash book control
802 : debtors control
901 : VAT control

The salient details of our three transactions are:

- TRANSACTION A

  Sales invoice no : 10001
  Account : AAR001 (Aardvark and Co)
  Gross amount : £470
  VAT amount : £70

  Nominal analysis
  Sales of product A (code 101) : £300
  Sales of product B (code 102) : £100

- TRANSACTION B

  Sales invoice no : 10002
  Account : AAR001 (Aardvark and Co)
  Gross amount : £235
  VAT amount : £35

  Nominal analysis
  Sales of product A (code 101) : £200

- TRANSACTION C

  Cash receipt (payment of invoice 10001)
  Account : AAR001 (Aardvark and Co)
  Net amount : £470
  Discount taken : £0

  Nominal analysis
  Cash book control (code 801) : £470

Assuming that transactions A and B are entered in the same batch of sales invoices to the sales ledger, then they would progress through our imaginary system as follows.

Input of sales invoices

The first step would be the input of transactions A and B in a batch of sales invoices (eg batch number I001) such that they are recorded on the sales batch file (SBF). The bare detail of the records on the SBF would appear something like:

ACCOUNT	REF	VALUE	NET	NOMINAL ANALYSIS
AAR001	10001	470	70	901 (VAT control)
AAR001	10001	0	300	101 (Sales product A)
AAR001	10001	0	100	102 (Sales product B)
AAR001	10002	235	35	901 (VAT control)
AAR001	10002	0	200	101 (Sales product A)

In reality, there would also be other data contained within each record (eg batch number, invoice date, period number, remarks, etc) but the above is sufficient to illustrate a skeleton of the processing involved. Note also that this is by no means the only way in which transactions may be held by a system and this is not, therefore, 'how computers do it' but rather 'how computers might do it'.

Posting to sales ledger

We can now run the sales ledger posting routine to get the two sales invoices on to the sales ledger. Hence the records for £470 and £235 would be added to the sales ledger file (SLF) (as debits) for account AAR001 and as a credit to the control account record (eg Account ZZZZZZ) added for the overall value of the posting, ie:

ACCOUNT	REF	VALUE
AAR001	10001	470
AAR001	10002	235
ZZZZZZ	Batch I001	–705

Note that there is no need for the nominal analysis to be held on the sales ledger nor, in strict terms, is the VAT element required, providing that it is available elsewhere in the system. Nevertheless, some systems include the VAT element on the sales ledger record as it is occasionally required by users to be shown on customer statements. Note also how the addition of the internal control account record makes it easy for the system to determine whether the file is in balance, ie the sum of all the transactions on the file is zero.

Sales ledger posting – update of other files

In addition to adding records to SLF, as described above, the ledger posting routine would also need to update the memorandum balance field on the customer master file (CMF) for both accounts AAR001 and the control account. Turnover figures on this file would also be updated by the net (ie VAT exclusive) value of the transactions so that, in this example, the turnover figure for customer AAR001 would be increased by £600.

Having dealt with the sales ledger files, the posting operation would also need to add records to:

- the day book file (DBF);
- the sales VAT reporting file (VRF); and
- the nominal postings file (NPF).

In practice, elements of these files may be combined and even the initial sales batch file may be used as the basis of the day book print if batches can be 'frozen' (ie can no longer be amended) on the file after they have been posted to the ledger. For the day book and VAT reporting functions, sufficient information must be passed to the respective files to enable adequate reports to be obtained and the files will be subject to different rules for clearance, the day book file probably being cleared down at the end of each period, whereas the VAT reporting file may be required to retain information at least on a quarterly basis.

Input of cash receipt

Transaction C involves receipt of the customer's cheque in respect of the invoice for £470 and this receipt would be entered to the sales cash input file (SCF) through the cash input stream and, at some stage, allocated against the invoice to which it relates. Although there is only the one transaction in this example, this entry would normally comprise part of batch (eg batch number C001). The input would look like:

ACCOUNT	REF	VALUE
AAR001	Cash	–470

Posting of cash to sales ledger

The cash on SCF would then be used to create further records on the sales ledger (SLF) so that this would then appear as:

ACCOUNT	REF	VALUE
AAR001	10001	470 X
AAR001	10002	235
ZZZZZZ	Batch I001	–705
AAR001	Cash	–470 X
ZZZZZZ	Batch C001	470

(The 'X' denotes the transactions which have been allocated against each other.)

Note that the sum of the values on the ledger is still zero as the control account records form a self-balancing control on the file. Hence, if a record became lost or corrupted at any point in the file (ie not necessarily in the vicinity of the new records which have been added), perhaps due to hardware or media error, then this would be found when the integrity of the file was next checked (ie when the whole of the file is summed) wherever in the file the fault may lie.

The postings routine in respect of cash transactions would require the current balance field on the customer master file to be downdated by the value of the receipt for customer AAR001 (and similarly for the control account record on CMF), but note that there is no effect on turnover. Similarly, although there will still be the need to pass records to the nominal posting file, there would be no VAT reporting requirement and, depending upon the system, the records may not be required on a day book reporting file.

The nominal postings file

Assuming that there is no summarization of nominal transactions in operation, the nominal postings file (NPF) will now have the following appearance in respect of the sales ledger transactions detailed above. Even if entries to the nominal ledger are to be summarized, the nominal postings file may still be retained in a detailed form in order to substantiate the trail of transactions through the system to the nominal ledger and, in any case, it may also be used for other purposes.

NOMINAL CODE	REF	VALUE
901	10001	–70
101	10001	–300
102	10001	–100
901	10002	–35
101	10002	–200
802	Batch I001	705
801	Batch C001	470
802	Batch C001	–470

Note first the signs of the amounts; the analysis of the sales invoices are negative so that, using the convention which we have adopted, the amounts are treated as credits on the nominal ledger. The sum of the values for the whole file is zero which, of course, is only a computerized way of saying that the total of the debit postings equals those of the credits.

Nominal ledger posting

In this scenario the nominal ledger posting routine may merely involve the transfer of unposted records from the NPF on to the nominal ledger (NLF), assuming that no summarization of the transactions is to be carried out. Although the records would normally be added chronologically, the file would be indexed (as would the sales and purchase ledger files) so that it could be accessed and processed with the records in nominal code order if required. In this form it would appear as follows:

NOMINAL CODE	REF	VALUE
101	10001	–300
101	10002	–200
102	10001	–100
801	Batch C001	470
802	Batch I001	705
802	Batch C001	–470
901	10001	–70
901	10002	–35

In effect, this file is a replica of the double entry accounts which could have been produced by our three transactions, ie:

	DR	CR
101 : sales of product A		
Invoice 1001		300
Invoice 1002		200
102 : sales of product B		
Invoice 1001		100
801 : cash book control		
Cash batch C001	470	
802 : debtors control		
Invoice batch I001	705	
Cash batch C001		470
901 : VAT control		
Invoice 1001		70
Invoice 1002		35

Hopefully, this will help to 'debunk' some of the mysteries of computerized accounting as, in the end, we have ended up with accounts produced to the same rules as those by traditional methods. As already noted, it is the means by which the accounts are maintained which are different, but not the underlying principles of the accounts themselves.

Reminder

Remember to take the above only as an example of how things could happen and not necessarily how they do occur in any one system, but the overall principle of processing, while deliberately simplistic, is perfectly valid. Individual systems will vary markedly, for example in respects such as:

- whether the ledgers are updated in batch or 'real time' mode (ie whether the ledger posting process is effectively incorporated within the transaction entry process);
- the degree of summarization, if any, for the posting of sales and purchase transactions to the nominal ledger;
- the treatment of cash entries, particularly the processing of allocations against outstanding invoices;
- the source and method used for the production of day book and VAT reports.

Additionally, integration with other modules in the software, such as sales invoicing and stock control, may introduce other constraints upon the way processing is carried out, as will the degree of further analysis required, particularly from the sales and purchase ledger systems.

PART 2

BEFORE IMPLEMENTATION

4

Preparing the Way

A LONG AND TORTUOUS JOURNEY

It is possible to buy a full accounting software system costing thousands of pounds. Equally it is possible to purchase one for less than a hundred pounds or, indeed, for almost any figure between these two extremes. Will there be any difference between all these products? Well, you would certainly expect there to be so, although price is by no means the only indicator of quality or range of facilities. It does, however, serve to illustrate the diversity of products available to satisfy what are essentially the same set of requirements. This in turn indicates the care which needs to be taken before embarking upon the implementation route.

Other than the approximate budget which you are prepared to allocate to the exercise, the most important element of the selection process is the definition of the facilities (hopefully to become benefits) anticipated as a result of the new regime. If this sounds obvious, it is still the case that many users fail to define their requirements, even in the most global of terms, at the outset and it is therefore hardly surprising that there are so many systems which fail to live up to their expectations. The reality is that implementing an accounting system can sometimes be a long and tortuous journey, but it is a considerable advantage to know in advance:

- precisely where you are going, and
- how much the fare is.

The selection decision should be more than saying 'I think we'll computerize our accounts', even if it is only to add 'when I have time to deal with it' as an afterthought. Not that preparing the way should be a particularly lengthy or onerous task. Unless you have requirements which are likely to be very specific to your particular operation there is little point in compiling a lengthy specification of what is needed. For one thing, few people other than yourself will bother to read it in any degree of detail and, for another, if what you need really requires a lengthy specification then you will probably be looking to commission your own bespoke system.

More useful and manageable is a list of broad headings of facilities which can be denoted as 'essentials' and 'desirables' in terms of the system you require, ie the 'where you are going' element of the journey. Some people, by their nature, will tend to put more items in the essentials column than in the desirables; this is fine, but they will need to remember that the more the list is weighted in this way, the less chance there will be of finding a standard product which will satisfy it and the more chance there will be that the 'fare' for the journey will be markedly increased as a consequence.

To settle any doubts, for the purposes of this chapter the following definitions can apply.

Essential

A facility without which the system will be inoperable in your environment.

Desirable

A facility without which the system will be less than perfect, but will still be operable.

It really is as simple as that. The most essential 'essential' of all of course is that the system should keep proper accounting records, a basic fact which is often forgotten in the unremitting quest for bells and whistles. Other factors which may come into the 'essentials' column include:

- specific coding structures and conventions, particularly for nominal account codes;
- size of critical fields;
- multi-company operation;
- multi-currency operation;
- multi-user operation;
- integration with other modules and packages;
- reporting, and report writing, facilities;
- other company specific requirements.

There may also be particular facilities within each module which may be vital in your eyes such as, for example, the ability of the purchase ledger to produce cheques automatically in respect of payments made or a nominal ledger facility for standard journals to deal with items which recur from period to period. Whatever is required, a little thought at the start of the exercise can go a long way and this chapter should provide some pointers in the right direction. Remember that, with an accounting system, you may have to live with your mistakes for a long time and you will probably be reminded of them daily.

SCOPE OF COMPUTERIZATION

The phrase 'accounting system' has been used in this book to denote the three principal ledgers, ie sales, purchase and nominal. By their nature, these systems are merely recording events which have already taken place and the rest of the business carries on around, or rather before, them. In practice, therefore, the implementation of an accounting system is likely to take place in tandem with some of these related elements of the business operation such as sales invoicing, sales order processing, stock control, purchase order processing and payroll. In fact, for many organizations, some of these 'peripheral' systems form the main focus of the implementation with the ledgers being relegated almost to the status of incidental, albeit necessary, additions. It is not difficult to see why this should often be the case. The receipt and recording of sales orders, their fulfilment from stock and the invoicing of goods delivered form the lifeblood of a commercial organization's well- being. The efficiency of the order handling and delivery operations will be instrumental in shaping customers' perceptions and the accuracy and timeliness of invoices will be vital to cash flow. None of these activities is directly dependent upon the operation of the ledgers although any deficiencies in the ledger systems will eventually impact adversely upon the main business thrust.

The scope of computerization is, therefore, one of the most critical decisions to be made at the start of the project. Even if it is not intended to start with invoicing and order processing options, if it is likely that they will be required in the future then the remit of the search for accounting software must include the brief that it is 'backwards compatible' with acceptable software in these areas.

It is also now possible to think on a much less parochial scale about accounting systems. The open systems concept which looks set to embrace the computing community is likely to mean that the possibilities which are already afforded for the transfer of data between systems and packages will continue to increase. This will mean that further opportunities will be presented for those who appreciate that accounting data forms an integral part of an organization's overall information and that it is not necessarily something which has to be jealously guarded as 'property of the accounts department'. This does not imply that there will be unrestricted access for all (although the more 'open' an open system, the more consideration must be given to security), but that the data, probably in a summarized form, can be directly interfaced with other systems, perhaps running on different machines and operating environments.

FACILITIES WITHIN THE MODULES

There is a temptation, particularly among the unversed in such matters, to think that one package of a particular type is the same as another, for example that a purchase ledger from company X is the same as that from company Y. While it is true that you would expect them to have some similarity in terms of functions (it would be disappointing, for example, if either did not allow a purchase ledger to be maintained!) it is quite possible that the range of facilities will differ markedly. To some extent you are likely to get what you pay for; a package costing £50 will certainly manage less (although possibly not proportionately so) than a package costing £500. This is not to say that the £50 package may not be suitable in particular circumstances, in fact having too many facilities can be just as much of an encumbrance as having too few, particularly when these facilities slow down input, processing and reporting and require more in the way of disk storage space.

In broad terms, the accounting systems marketplace has been split into the following pricing sectors:

- budget;
- mid-range;
- top end;

and the number and sophistication of facilities incorporated are likely to vary as one moves up the spectrum. In any event, whatever the facilities a particular system may possess, the basic requirement of maintaining proper accounting records should never be forgotten.

The precise facilities required from a system will naturally vary between specific users but some of the more common critical elements are set out below. Remember that not all systems will include all these facilities and, if it is intended to pursue a purely packaged approach to implementation (ie there are to be no amendments to the basic product purchased), then a certain level of compromise may need to be accepted. In this respect, the accurate distillation of 'essentials' from 'desirables' becomes a fundamental part of the selection process. Among the principal selection criteria are the following.

General

- integration between ledgers and other related modules;
- multi-company operation;
- multi-user operation;
- multi-currency operation;
- size and format of fields;
- types of transactions permitted;
- reporting for VAT purposes;
- general scope and flexibility of reporting and enquiries;
- generation of user specified reports;
- ability of ledgers to be in different periods;
- adequacy of controls implemented;
- availability of management information;
- import or export of data to or from 'foreign' systems;
- speed of operation (particularly if large volumes are anticipated).

Purchase ledger

- size and format of supplier account code;
- purchase invoice registration facilities;
- nominal analysis capabilities;
- automated payment procedures;
- handling of cash discounts available;
- cheque writing and remittance advice note production;
- transfer of payments using BACS.

Sales ledger

- □ size and format of customer account code;
- □ selective label printing of customer names and addresses;
- □ customization of statement layout and content;
- □ generation of user composed debtors letters;
- □ basis and method of ageing analysis;
- □ customer and turnover analysis facilities;
- □ ancillary analysis fields provided.

Nominal ledger

- □ size and format of nominal code;
- □ cost centre or department analysis facilities;
- □ handling of accruals and prepayments;
- □ facility for entry of 'standard' journals;
- □ budgetary control facilities;
- □ flexible profit and loss and balance sheet reporting;
- □ other management reports;
- □ number of accounting periods available;
- □ financial year-end facilities;
- □ consolidation facilities between companies;
- □ transfer of data to and from other systems.

It is worth taking a closer look at some of the major environmental factors, starting with the projected data volumes and their implications.

VOLUMES

In the days when most systems were based upon floppy disk storage or low capacity (eg less than 20Mb) hard disks, the volumes with which an accounting system needed to cope were critical when selecting hardware and software. Some software was limited in its ability to cope with high volumes, perhaps because of restrictions in the size of the account number field or other internal limitations whereas the more sophisticated systems had larger program libraries and data files resulting in a greater need for disk storage. Most of these worries had receded by the end of the 1980s. Not that the problems caused by running out of disk storage space are any less painful but rather because higher capacity drives are readily available there is less excuse for sailing so close to the wind.

Even so, it is useful to have some idea of the likely capacity requirement of a system and some software suppliers may be able to tell you this with the help of some information on your projected volumes. The critical volumes for this sort of exercise are likely to be those relating to:

- □ number of customer accounts;

- number of supplier accounts;
- number of nominal codes and cost centres;
- number of sales/purchase invoices per period;
- number of nominal journals per period;
- number of outstanding sales/purchase invoices at period end;
- the frequency with which each ledger is to be cleared down, ie allocated transactions are to be removed from the sales/purchase ledgers and consolidated balances brought forward in the nominal ledger;
- scope of budgetary information (eg a system enabling monthly budgets to be set for each cost centre or department within each nominal code would be likely to require a large file for this purpose).

In assessing transactions, remember to allow for an increase in volumes over the lifetime of the system. Similarly, the master files will generally not only contain those customers and suppliers with whom you are actively dealing at any point in time (the number of which may be quite small), but also those which are 'dormant', the records for which are likely to take up as much space as those which are live. A better way to approach these projected volumes, therefore, is to assess how many different customers or suppliers are likely to be dealt with over, say, a three-year period. This would allow for customers and suppliers with whom there has been trade in the current year or the two previous years to be retained on file but would assume that any older records would be deleted and the space reclaimed.

Having arrived at some projected volumes, take great care in making assumptions as to the disk capacity required for such data. This will vary markedly between different software depending upon factors such as:

- the record sizes used for individual data files;
- whether fixed or variable length records are used;
- whether space is automatically reclaimed when records are deleted;
- whether sales/purchase ledger transactions are summarized in any way when posted to the nominal ledger;
- the use of archive files for old transactions;
- the presence of detailed analysis files (eg sales by product by customer by month).

It is also essential to note that it is not only the size of the principal data files (ie master files and ledgers) which need to be considered but also the program library (the more sophisticated the system, the larger the program library is likely to be) and other data files such as:

- transaction input files, (eg for batches awaiting posting to the ledger);
- memorandum files (eg for VAT reporting);
- internal work files (eg as may be created during end of period routines);
- parameter files (eg for holding global system details such as your organization's name and address);
- analysis files;
- index files required for facilities such as account number look up on master files, etc;

- ancillary files, such as report definitions, text files, etc.

All of these may amount to a considerable overhead and, given that the incremental cost of hardware in acquiring a system with a larger hard disk capacity is normally relatively small, it is nearly always worthwhile to 'trade yourself up', particularly if the system is also to be used for other applications.

NUMBER OF USERS

The number of users who are to have access to the system is a prime consideration in terms of hardware and operating system selection as well as dictating the applications software to be used. Advances in hardware technology mean that it is now possible for users of microcomputers to choose between a networked method of operation (in which a number of computers are linked together, sharing a hard disk file server on one of them) or a true multi-user concept (in which a number of dumb terminals are linked to a single computer) or, indeed, a combination of the two.

Whatever method is adopted in principle, from an applications viewpoint, you will need to ensure that any proposed software is not only available in a multi-user form (the 'multi-user' here denotes the characteristic of the software), but that it will be warrantied to run in the specific network or multi-user operating environment which is adopted. Not all accounting software packages are available in a multi-user version and those which are will be fairly specific about the types of environment in which they will perform. Even if you are about to embark upon a single-user route, if there is any possibility that the system may later need to be upgraded to multi-user operation, the feasibility and implications need to be borne in mind from the outset unless, that is, you do not mind the possibility of having to change software as well when the time arrives.

Multi-user accounting software has been available for microcomputer systems for some years although it must be said that some early implementations were less than robust. The difference between single and multi-user software relates principally to the need for the software to provide protection for data when it is being updated by a particular user. Two users simultaneously trying to perform a ledger update, for example, would lead to grief if both were permitted to write to the file irrespective of the needs of the other. For this reason concepts such as file locking (where the whole file is locked by a user while a particular operation is effected) and record locking (in which the lock is restricted to the individual record being worked on by the user) are utilized to control access by users. While the operation of such locking should be transparent to the user (other than, of course, the messages relating to unsuccessful attempts to gain access to a particular facility or record), the flexibility in terms of multiple usage of the system can vary considerably between systems, as the locks employed by one system can be very much more restrictive than those imposed by another. For most circumstances, the ability for transactions to be entered concurrently, and within the same ledger, by a number of users is the prime concern but whatever the criteria in terms of multi-user operation these should be checked specifically with the supplier of the proposed system.

Other considerations relating to the acquisition of multi-user software include the following:

- □ What are the cost, licence and support implications of multi-user software as against the single-user version?
- □ What is the maximum number of users which may be accommodated by the software?
- □ How are additional users added? Can this be effected by the user or must there be recourse to the supplier or software house?
- □ Are further charges payable when further users are added?

While many in any case consider a visit to a reference site a vital part of the selection process, it is particularly useful for a multi-user system. Not only can the effect of the locking in 'live' action can be seen, but some idea of the response and processing times that are likely to apply with reasonable sized data files and other users on the system can be gauged. Having said this, any differences between the hardware proposed and that on view should also be taken into account in the assessment of performance.

On a more cautionary note, the adoption of a multi-user system brings with it far more in the way of responsibilities with regard to matters such as security of access, control over operations and housekeeping duties. There is little doubt that there is far more that can go wrong, not only in terms of the accounting software itself, but problems consequent upon failure of one of the hardware elements of the system. For the 'beginner' in computing or accounting this can all be rather daunting (not to mention depressing) and there is much to be said for at least starting off with a single-user system to gain some basic experience.

INTEGRATION WITH OTHER MODULES AND SYSTEMS

Integration with other systems has increased in importance when selecting a system. Within the three ledger systems themselves it would be expected that there would be a seamless and smooth integration between the purchase/sales ledgers and the nominal. It is also possible that each of the ledger systems may also need to interface with other modules from the same software house or, more unusually, with systems which are not directly compatible, some work having been done by one or other of the software writers to effect an interface. Typical interfaces would be as follows.

Sales ledger

- □ sales invoicing (and thence sales order processing);
- □ stock control (and thence bill of materials and materials requirements planning);
- □ nominal ledger;
- □ customer marketing/sales analysis system.

Purchase ledger

- purchase order processing;
- stock control;
- nominal ledger.

Nominal ledger

- sales ledger;
- purchase ledger;
- stock control (for closing stock journal in a fully integrated system);
- payroll;
- fixed assets accounting;
- 'cash book'.

Not all users require all, or necessarily any, of the above interfaces, but even where implementations are restricted initially to the ledger systems it will be useful to know what possibilities are readily available for widening the scope of the computerization at a later stage. If the software you are acquiring does not have one of your potential modules in its current product range then you may well experience a problem by pursuing that software unless there is a convincing reason to do so. With an eye on costs, it may be possible to make some savings through the 'bundling' of modules if they are all purchased at one time (irrespective of whether they are to be used) rather than making separate purchases (at 'stand alone' prices) as time goes on.

On a wider front, there is an increasing requirement for accounting software to integrate easily with other types of systems, either for further manipulation or analysis of the basic data, or for display and presentation purposes. Here are some examples of such interfaced systems.

Spreadsheet and modelling systems

These are typically linked with a nominal ledger for flexible manipulation of trial balance or budgetary data and for refining management reports. Such systems also enable projections to be evaluated on the basis of existing data and, depending upon the system in use, for the graphical output of data. Many accounting systems recognize the need for this interface, some by enabling output of a file which can be read in by a specified spreadsheet. Most spreadsheet packages will in any case allow for the 'import' of files held in a variety of standard data formats.

Graphics packages

Output in a graphical form can be further refined by the use of specific purpose graphics packages. The use of high resolution colour screens has now become commonplace as have quality definition printers and such advances make the time invested in graphical presentation well worthwhile.

Word processing

Word processing will be used perhaps for letters to be sent to recalcitrant debtors or indeed for any general mailshot to customers or suppliers. What is required is an easy link between data held on the master file (including, naturally, names and addresses) and a proprietary word processing package.

Word processing also has its use in the preparation of final accounts for external distribution, the figures from the accounts system generally being transferred to a compatible text file. This text file can then be accessed by the WP package for the addition of further narrative and for formatting and design.

Desktop publishing (DTP)

For a really smart appearance many organizations now utilize DTP facilities for the distribution of accounting information. Such systems are often flexible in their methods of data capture, including that of graphical images, and offer new possibilities for the creative accountant (if not for creative accounting!).

Other forms of interface are instanced when the three ledgers are not from the same software stable and/or are not being run at the same location. It is not uncommon for, say, the sales and purchase ledgers to be interfaced with a nominal ledger of a 'foreign' system. This may arise for example where geographically localized units may perform their own sales or purchase ledger accounting, the results of which are to be processed by a national system running at the organization's headquarters. In this situation not only are there the normal perils of managing the interface with the nominal ledger to consider, but also how the nominal postings data is to be controlled and transferred between sites and machines including possible changes in data format and operating system.

Multi-company operation

The operation of separate ledgers for more than one company is a common requirement and one which will be dealt with by many accounting packages. As well as being used within an organization for companies under its remit, it also can provide a ready-made means for those who run a bureau type of service for a number of clients. One way in which a multi-company approach could be accommodated would be to implement the whole system (ie including a separate implementation of the program library) discretely for each separate company, assuming that this would be permitted by the package. This would not be the best of routes, however, as it would imply:

- wastage of hard disk resources through having separate copies of the program library resident;
- any consolidation or linking between companies would presumably be precluded.

Ideally, multi-company operation should permit each company to be accessed from within the same menu structure and it is obviously vital that all displays and reports should clearly identify to which company they relate. Some systems provide for the nominal chart of accounts to be copied from an existing company to one which has been newly set up, an excellent time-saving facility if common nominal codes are in operation throughout. On a related front, the provision of a consolidated (or, to be more precise, aggregated) trial balance and management reports (eg profit and loss and balance sheet) can be expected. In a similar fashion to multi-user systems, the following questions might usefully be asked at an early stage.

- ☐ What are the cost, licence and support implications of having multiple companies?
- ☐ What is the maximum number of companies which can be accommodated in any one implementation?
- ☐ Can new companies be created by the user without further recourse to the supplier or software house?
- ☐ What level of integration or consolidation is available between different companies?

Other than appreciating the need for the additional disk storage space required and the potential for entering the data for one company accidentally into another (the threat of which can be reduced by ensuring that entirely different supplier and customer account codes are used within each company), there are few dangers inherent in multi-company processing. It is important, however, to be aware of the implications for taking backup copies of data. Ideally, it should be possible to take a backup copy solely of one company if so required and, perhaps more importantly, selectively restore the data for that company from an archive without affecting the data for any of the other companies.

Multi-currency operation

Multi-currency accounting is becoming an increasingly common requirement as markets and operations expand internationally. Multi-currency systems tend, almost of necessity, to be concentrated at the more sophisticated end of the marketplace and this is another area where the descriptive phrase tends to mean all things to all people whereas, in practice, users' requirements can vary widely. For example, some may want a multi-currency purchase ledger, but want the sales and nominal ledgers to be processed purely in sterling. Others may require that a multi-company and multi-currency environment is instituted in which, say, there is one company with sterling ledgers, another with dollars, another with yen, and so on. The consolidation process in such instances, whereby a combined set of accounts is produced in a single 'target' currency, requires particularly careful thought, especially if different exchange rates are to be applied to, say, balance sheet items (perhaps a 'snapshot' exchange rate for end of period balances) and profit and loss items (perhaps a temporal exchange rate relating to transactions in the period to which they relate).

The setting of exchange rates for the different currencies processed by the system and the timing of the application of exchange rates to transactions and/

or balances are further likely areas of dissimilarities between potential users. The mechanism for coping with exchange differences will also need to be established to ensure that it is in accordance with requirements. Such exchange differences will result, for example, when a currency sales invoice, converted to sterling at the time of posting to the ledger, is paid in the native currency, which is converted at a different rate reflecting the different point in time of the transaction.

There is another piece of advice for nervous beginners to accounting systems. If foreign currencies form only a small percentage of overall accounting transactions, it may be worth proceeding with a single currency (ie sterling) system with any currency conversion calculations being effected outside the system and recorded on the relevant source documents. While this may sound somewhat Luddite in concept, it does mean that the mainstream of work is likely to be processed more easily, and the complications (not to mention the extra key depressions required) of the multi-currency approach can be avoided or at least delayed until more familiarity and confidence with systems can be gained.

As a final warning, beware of the difficulties which may be posed by some currencies, such as the lira and the yen, in which the units are invariably high, possibly leading to difficulties with numeric field overflows or loss of precision in calculations, particularly in systems which have obviously been designed for the smaller enterprise. While systems which cater specifically for such currencies should cope well, problems may be experienced when, for example, a single currency (sterling) ledger package is used for maintaining ledgers in one of these currencies, perhaps as part of a multi-company set-up.

SPECIFIC REQUIREMENTS

All the facilities described thus far are likely to be included in standard software packages but not all are necessarily to be found within the same one. There often comes a point, however, where users consider that they have requirements which cannot be satisfied through a standard system. The pros and cons of modified (or tailored) and specific (or bespoke) software are debated in Chapter 5 but, unless you like a hard life, always think carefully before deviating from standard products. At the very least, the amendments being considered should realistically be on your 'essentials' list in terms of requirements from the system. A 'desirable' facility, however 'desirable' it may be, may well not be worth the delay in implementation, increase in cost, weakening of the basic product and potential problems in support and upgrading which may ensue.

In the event, many amendments are driven not so much by the need to change the ledger systems but by the more user specific areas such as sales order processing, stock control and sales invoicing. These requirements often relate to such aspects as the layout of despatch note and invoice documentation and to additional fields or modes of processing which may be required to accommodate the normal practices of particular trades and industries. A jeweller, for example, may have certain requirements regarding the calculation of the selling price of products containing gold and in the way that such items are to be shown on sales invoices. A completely different set of requirements can be anticipated for, say, a builders' merchant.

These variations in the requirements of users in different industries are frequently catered for by vertical market accounting software which address the specific processing requirements which are likely to apply. Such products are often the outcome of a project carried out initially for one organization in the industry and have been generalized to widen their appeal to other firms in that market. If you find that your requirements are not easily satisfied by the general off-the-shelf packages which are available for accounting systems then it is worthwhile turning your attention to such products, although you should recognize that you are likely to end up paying more for such software in the long run. Trade associations, publications and exhibitions are good sources for tracking down such systems and, of course, any reference site is likely to be in a similar position to your own; it could even turn out to be one of your main competitors! If your choice is very much driven by the requirements of the 'peripheral' modules it is still important to appreciate that the same criteria still need to apply to the accounting elements of the system, particularly those relating to control.

INVOLVEMENT OF EXTERNAL ADVISERS

If you are neither an accountant (and many people who successfully implement accounting systems have no formal accountancy qualification) nor consider yourself computer-literate, then it will almost certainly pay you to seek some advice before committing yourself too far. In the microcomputer market there is often some reluctance to do this as, given the relatively low price of the hardware and software, users tend to shy away from the prospect of paying what seems in comparison to be high consultancy or advisory fees. In answer to this, do reconsider the list of things that can go wrong in Chapter 1. If you buy the 'wrong' word processor or spreadsheet you can doubtless shrug your shoulders and put it down to experience; the wrong accounting system, however, will prove to be a millstone from which it will be more difficult and, it has to be said, expensive to break free.

A natural place to turn is to your own accountants, who are likely to have equipped themselves to a greater or lesser degree in advising and assisting their clients in respect of computerization. They will almost certainly have evaluated some of the major software packages and will prove invaluable in assisting you in drawing up your list of 'essentials' and 'desirables'; indeed, they are quite likely to have some ready-made questionnaires to help with the exercise. It is, after all, your accountants who will have to live with some of the consequences of your decision although it is always worth remembering that it is you, and not they, who will be running the system for three hundred and sixty-five days of the year. Nevertheless, even if you do not wish to involve them in your selection and implementation processes, it is courteous to advise them of the change as they may wish to familiarize themselves with the system before the pressure of the audit is upon them.

Other avenues of approach include consultants, computer dealers and business acquaintances. It is impossible to make generalizations as to the worth of guidance given by any one category but you should always look beyond the advice given to gauge the following.

- The likely degree of objectivity, eg is the adviser on a commission arrangement for the recommendation of any particular product?
- The level of experience (both computing and accounting) behind the advice.
- Whether the advice relates to a tried and tested (and perhaps rather old?) system or to a new (and perhaps less robust and unproven?) product. It is easy for advisers to recommend 'what they know' which can be both good and bad news in a marketplace which moves so rapidly. There can also be dangers in listening to people who recommend 'what they have heard about', as some product announcements are months, if not occasionally years, ahead of the arrival of the products themselves!
- The level of actual (and practical) exposure to the advised product, eg is this a product which is well known to the adviser, having been involved in its implementation or operation, or is the experience gained through word of mouth?

At this stage you are looking for advice in terms of defining your needs, but as events progress you may also require assistance in selecting a product and even in its implementation. Having got to this stage, however, you should now be ready to face the world and look for what you want and this exciting venture is covered in the next chapter.

5

Selecting the Route

GOING SHOPPING

Having defined what is expected of a system, or at least having drawn up a broad list of 'essential' and 'desirable' facilities, you will have arrived at the stage at which you can at last go shopping. Before getting the carrier bags ready, however, it is worth pausing to think exactly where you are going or, rather, what it is you will be looking for. After the initial evaluation exercise you may already have some idea as to whether your requirements are likely to be easily met by a number of products or whether someone is going to have to do some programming work specifically for you. This is an important distinction as, in essence, there are three routes for the acquisition of accounting software. These are:

- purchasing an off-the-shelf product (packaged software);
- purchasing an off-the-shelf package with some modifications specific to your requirements (tailored software);
- commissioning a system to your requirements (bespoke software).

In fact these options are not always as clear cut as they may seem, as there are various shades of grey between the black and white choices. An off-the-shelf package may be altered only very slightly (eg the provision of an additional file listing type of report), such that, for all intents and purposes, it can be considered as the base product. Conversely, a bespoke system will rarely be started from scratch but will have elements of the ledger programs as a base from which much of the programming and systems definition commences. Nevertheless, considering each of these three avenues of approach provides a convenient split for the purposes of comparison.

Accounting systems are in some ways different from other systems in that there is already a large (and seemingly ever-growing) market of ready-made general purpose packages just waiting for prospective users. A recent publication, aimed at accountants, noted that it had details of twelve *thousand* relevant products on file although, admittedly, not all related merely to ledger systems. Even if the general purpose ledger packages are not sufficient there is also quite an army of industry specific accounting products (ie vertical market packages) which combine the accounting elements with that industry's more specific invoicing or record-keeping requirements. It is surprising, therefore, that so many organizations find their accounting requirements are *so* special that they need to have software modified or written for them. In truth, many of these modifications are likely to centre around the invoicing, order processing or stock control elements rather than the ledgers but, as many of these alterations may impact on, say, the customer master file their effect tends to work its way through to the ledger systems.

Note that all of this has been covered without the consideration of hardware. It is, of course, impossible to deal with the applications software entirely in isolation of the likely hardware environment and, in truth, there are few selection procedures which do not proceed without some specific piece of equipment in mind. It is as well, however, to try to keep these considerations as far to the back of the mind as possible until the software route has been defined. Unless you are working under a policy of buying a particular manufacturer's equipment or are making use of existing kit, look at hardware after you have found your software, not the other way round.

PACKAGED SOFTWARE

As noted, there are more off-the-shelf software packages available for accounting systems than for any other application. While it is true that, by definition, there must be some similarity between them (they are all, after all, purporting to do broadly the same job), it would be a mistake to think that they are all the same: far from it. While there may be similarities in the mainstream ledger maintenance functions (although there is quite some scope for these to be handled in differing ways) and purely cosmetic differences in screen layouts and reporting, there are many facilities which differentiate between competing products. Some of these were identified in Chapter 4.

If you have done your homework properly, you will be clear that the features in your 'essentials' list are, indeed, essential and you can focus your attention on these in the initial selection phase. Many users start from the viewpoint that there cannot be a standard package which will meet all their requirements (ie 'desirables' as well as 'essentials') and, therefore, there will be some need for programming specific to them. This is of course likely to be true; a packaged product which has been written for general use rather than for a particular circumstance is unlikely to fulfil *all* the requirements of *all* the users. It may, however, fulfil all the requirements of some users and some of the requirements of all users. It is worth establishing where you stand in relation to this framework as it is normally far better to adopt the standard product if at all possible.

Not the least reason for this is financial. The standard package will invariably cost far less than any form of product which is customized to requirements. The economics of packaged software production are that the labour intensive front-end costs of specification, coding, testing and documenting are, hopefully, recovered in the medium term (long term being unlikely to happen in the fast moving (or, rather, rapid obsolescence) computer business) by the volume of 'off-the-shelf' sales.

The amortization of development costs in this way, coupled with a competitive marketplace and a 'low cost' expectation of users of microcomputer systems, generally keeps prices down which is, of course, of benefit to the user although, as noted later, this has repercussions in the way that accounting software, in particular, is viewed by dealers. The low cost expectation frequently gears users to anticipate that the costs of modifications to packages will also be low, a view from which they are often rapidly dissuaded, as they discover at a later stage. In the end, you will be paying for a skilled person's time, something which is unlikely to come cheap.

There are other factors which weigh heavily in favour of using a standard package if at all possible and some of these are listed in the following section. If, however, you are still left with some of the 'essentials' on your list unsatisfied, then your next port of call is likely to be an investigation of the modification of an existing package to meet your needs, by a process often referred to as 'tailoring'.

TAILORED SOFTWARE

It may sound negative to say at the outset that the first question you should ask yourself when requesting modifications to a standard package is: 'Am I *absolutely* certain that there is no standard product which I can run acceptably?'

Think long and carefully before you reply because, once you have deviated from the path of standard packages you are entering a completely different world. If you are in any doubt, it may be worth seeing if you can run with the unmodified system first so that any changes are at least requested in the light of experience gained in practical operation.

Why be so cautious about changes? After all, there are no doubt countless users who are happily running modified versions of accounting systems. Well, without wishing to be too pessimistic, there are a number of ways in which modifications can cause difficulties, some of which are explained below.

Feasibility

First, are the modifications you require feasible in terms of the product? This may not always be obvious. Additional reports which use existing data are normally easily accommodated (although many packages now incorporate report writers for just this sort of requirement), but the addition of new fields or files is likely to pose greater problems. Software houses may in any case be reluctant to tamper with products beyond a certain extent or make modifications which upset the main processing and control principles of the system.

Source

That is, finding someone to do it. Not all producers of accounting software packages sanction changes and, even those that do will normally be selective about who they permit to do them. This is only fair as it is the name of their product which will suffer if a high level of customer dissatisfaction is raised through poor quality work by third parties. In any case, no one can make changes without authorized possession of the source code of the system. Your choices, therefore, may be limited.

Cost

The cost of amendments to packaged software is is quite likely to exceed the price of the basic package. This should not be too surprising; after all, among other things, you will be paying the charge-out cost of a programmer's time which will be paid at broadly the same rate as in a mainframe environment, even if the software is to be implemented on the cheapest microcomputer around.

Time

One of the beauties of a packaged product is that, having decided that you want it, it can be up and running on the same day. (At least that is the theory; the reality occasionally differs from this sublime concept!) Modifications, however, mean time. Even the most simple of amendments needs to be fitted into a production schedule and, if the software house is up to its eyes for the foreseeable future, then your system may arrive at some time in the less foreseeable future.

Testing

In Chapter 6, the testing of any accounting product is advocated, whatever its pedigree. For a standard package this is not so much to find major bugs but to make sure that all facilities are properly understood for the environment in which it is to operate. If the software has been in any way amended, however, the testing procedure will need to become more rigorous, again adding to the lead time associated with implementation. If problems are found with the modifications (and, depending what these are, they could manifest themselves in other parts of the system),then the process becomes even more drawn out, as will your nerves.

Maintenance and support

As soon as there is a departure from the standard product there arises a consequent increased risk in terms of ongoing maintenance and support, however good the intentions of the software house which carries out the work. The tailored parts of the system may be familiar only to a few people who, in the course of time, may leave the company and, even with the best systems and programming documentation, those that replace them may find the going difficult when fielding queries or dealing with further amendments.

Upgrades

From time to time most software companies revise their products in a major new release, normally incorporating enhancements over the previous products out in the field and, as it is in the interests of both parties, will often offer an upgrade to existing users at an attractive rate. Those users with modified systems may not be so easy to accommodate in such an arrangement, however, and it may not even be possible to upgrade the system at all, thus throwing a further burden on to the support task. In effect, depending upon the scale and nature of the modifications, there is a danger of there being an inbuilt obsolescence, a factor which is underlined when the mainstream software is upgraded to a newer version at a future date, leaving you dangerously perched on an increasingly unsupported (or unsupportable) product.

If all the above has not put you off, you will need to agree with the software house *precisely* what changes are required. Although most software houses are used to having to try their best, very few have authenticated powers of clairvoyancy, so you cannot expect enhancements which you have yet to think of to be incorporated, although a surprising number of users are disappointed when they find that this is not the case! When specifying amendments, be precise, be concise and be yourself. The latter refers to specifying amendments in your own terminology; do not think that because you are dealing with a computer company, you need to present them with a mountain of flow charts and references to specific file updates; they can work all this out for themselves. You can speak your language, they can speak theirs.

You are likely to want a fixed quotation for any modifications. If you think it unreasonably high, do not automatically begrudge the company concerned. Ask them what are the major factors contributing to the cost. Amendments which may sound simple to the layman (for example, an extra character for the customer account code) are often time-consuming to implement because of the number of programs affected rather than any inherent complexity of the requirement. It may be that you can, after all, live without some of the amendments and, again, the nearer you get to the standard product, the better. In any event, a fixed quotation is likely to include some contingency but you should recognize that any significant change to the scale of the amendments originally proposed is likely to result in a recosting.

As a final thought, it may be possible for some amendments to be incorporated outside the main system itself, perhaps being accessed by a stand-alone utility rather than through the main system menus. This approach would remove some of the projected disadvantages, particularly with respect to product upgrades, but it could realistically be used only for certain types of amendments, eg those such as special format reports or additional analysis processing outside the system. Further amendments may in any case need to be made if and when the main product is upgraded, but at least the core product remains untouched.

Where the level of amendment required is very high, you may be getting into the realms of commissioning your own system to be written. This is known as 'bespoke software'.

BESPOKE SOFTWARE

With bespoke systems, you really are on your own. You might end up with what you wanted, eventually, but you are likely to go through a whole gamut of emotions before the dust has settled. With ledger systems, you (or, rather, the software house) will rarely be starting from scratch; even if they do not market their own ledger systems they are likely to have some core routines available upon which they can build. With the number of packages on the market, it is unlikely that there are many organizations who really need their own ledger systems but, among the factors which may make it necessary, are complex and specific multi-currency requirements, special nominal coding requirements and unusual sales ledger or customer file recording requirements. As previously noted, in many cases, the driving force for the bespoke element of the systems will be the sales invoicing or sales order processing modules but, even if these requirements are specific, it may still be possible to bolt these on to relatively straightforward ledger modules and, if such a course is open, it is generally worth pursuing.

Like the process of birth, bespoke systems start as a gleam in someone's eye and, in the same vein, take some months (sometimes even years) of gestation before the product is brought (occasionally screaming) into the world. The analogy can be extended even further as the first few months of infancy are often the most troublesome and can bring the greatest strains on relationships!

Many of the considerations listed for tailored software apply equally, or even more so, for bespoke systems. Certainly, you will need a fairly specific document detailing your requirements and you will also need to find a software house that you not only find credible, but one with which you think you can work over the months ahead. This 'chemistry' between software house and user is of course a two-way process and its presence or absence indirectly accounts for the success or failure of many projects.

If this is your first venture into computing, it is well worth co-opting the help of someone who has been down this path before. Apart from guiding you along the way, it will help you to keep your expectations realistic (the more cynical would say pessimistic) and generally ensure that the right things happen in the right order and, hopefully, at the right time.

WHERE TO LOOK FOR ACCOUNTING PACKAGES

When you are ready to start shopping, where do you start to look? Well, you can try one or more of the following:

- books or directories;
- magazines;
- trade associations;
- exhibitions;
- computer dealers and software houses;
- demonstration disks;
- advisers, such as your accountants.

All the above can play their part in the selection and search for accounting software which perhaps explains why there is room for so many competing products in the marketplace. Different people have different preferences, but some considerations with regard to each approach follow.

Books and directories

There are various books and directories published from time to time which look at the principal accounting packages on the market and either list, or compare more deeply, the pertinent features of these products. Not only do such publications save hours of wading through advertising literature and dialogue with dealers, but they will also inform you of packages which you may not otherwise have known were available; not only that, you will probably also be provided with an initial contacts list. Armed with such a tome, you may even feel that you are able to draw up a shortlist without ever leaving your office, although you should take note of the age of the publication as many factors may have changed since it was published, not least the continuing existence of the software house or availability of the product! In a similar vein, the precise version number of the system being reviewed should also be noted.

Such publications are likely to give you the sort of useful information which is often difficult to find, such as how many installations there have been and, for example, whether there are any constraints as to the number of accounts which can be accommodated and so on. They are also likely to define the minimum hardware and operating system requirements and this can be an effective time-saver in matching packages to projected equipment.

Magazines

Looking through magazines is not as bad an idea as it may sound as they often contain brief directories of accounting products and, by their nature, they are likely to be reasonably topical. More importantly they will also occasionally include reviews of specific packages and, although these should be read with a degree of caution, remembering for instance that the reviewer may know little about the practicalities of running an accounts system, you should be able to pick up a general feel for the product. Another reason for caution is that the review products are occasionally 'beta test' or 'early release' versions of a forthcoming product, in which case the reviewer can go to town when something does not work quite as it should or when the product does not arrive with a completed glossy manual.

This does give a reminder that there is generally less risk involved in buying a tried and tested package rather than one which is 'hot off the press', although the additional features or 'state of the art' appearance of the latter may form a persuasive argument which is too strong to be ignored. Magazines are also useful sources of advertisements for both the accounting packages themselves and for dealers and many a search for software has actually begun at the newsagents' shelves.

Trade associations

Trade associations can also be useful reference points, particularly for industry specific products in vertical markets. While they may not point to specific recommendations, they should at least be able to furnish a list of potential suppliers as a starting point for gathering information.

Exhibitions

Exhibitions are marvellous places for exhibitors, but are frequently exhausting for the visitors. Some years ago there was a major computer exhibition virtually every week of the year but these have been steadily whittled down to a few remaining prestige events. For the prospective purchaser of accounting systems, exhibitions provide a good point of initial contact but cannot realistically be regarded as anything more. Unless the attendance is particularly low, it is unlikely that an exhibitor will wish to become involved in a detailed discussion or demonstration of a product and the exhibition environment is rarely conducive to clear thinking on either side. Nevertheless, exhibitions do provide a useful opportunity to 'get round' a number of products in a day and, perhaps even more importantly, to gain some insight into the people behind the companies.

Dealers and software houses

Your local High Street dealer may also be a useful starting point, although you should understand that what is likely to be recommended is what the dealer knows and sells and not necessarily what is best for you. You will also find that dealers vary considerably. Some may have little knowledge of, or even interest in, accounting systems whereas others may specialize in them. In the trade, the sale of accounting systems is generally regarded with some caution as it is recognized that such systems often entail a high degree of post-sales user support, some of which may relate to the understanding of accounting principles (and hence to the employment of specialist staff), rather than to computer related matters. The amount of pre-sales investment, at least in terms of time, also tends to be much higher than for other products and it is not uncommon for potential purchasers to require two, or even more, demonstrations before committing themselves. For this reason, many dealers fight shy of accounting systems or sell them on a 'cardboard box' basis. There is, of course, nothing wrong with this provided that it is made clear to any prospective purchaser from the outset.

An approach direct to a software house may also be worthwhile, although the larger suppliers will probably redirect your enquiry to the nearest dealer whom they have authorized to carry their product. Dealer authorization is not normally given lightly and any such dealer may have had to part with a significant investment in terms of money and time spent in training and product familiarization before being permitted to sell and support that particular software. All of this, of course, bodes well for the prospective customer.

External advisers

The use of external advisers, particularly firms of accountants, was introduced in Chapter 4 and, having gone past the initial definition of requirements, it may seem logical to continue the process into the selection of suitable software. For those who are effectively reliant on their accountants for financial information, they would in any case normally be the first port of call. Many accountancy firms now have specialists in computerized systems and they are likely to have dealt with and seen computerization in environments similar in size and operation to your own. Assuming that your accountant feels able to offer you advice it will undoubtedly be worth heeding, but remember that, wherever your advice comes from, it will in part be based on past experience and there may be newer products which are now worthy of your attention. Recommendations from business contacts or other sources can also be invaluable, particularly if they come direct from 'the horse's mouth' of a satisfied user of a particular system.

Demonstration disks

Demonstration disks of products, if available, can also be very useful, particularly in gauging the 'feel' of a system. These disks contain a subset of the package (eg with end of period facilities removed) or a package with a reduced limit of transactions or master file records which can be held. They provide you with an excellent opportunity to get the feel of a system and to get to grips with the reality of how it fits in with your own requirements. Not only that, you can also do this research in the privacy and convenience of your own office and at your own pace.

DEMONSTRATIONS

The net effect of all the above is likely to be an invitation to a demonstration of the product and this is often where the whole process takes a turn for the worse. Perhaps it is worth looking at why this should be so.

For the purchase of most accounting systems, the demonstration is the crunch point of the selection exercise, the point at which everything should fall into place and your decision-making process becomes a mere formality. The supplier will be eager to make a sale and you will be armed with your list of key points and questions. So why are demonstrations often so disappointing, both for buyer and seller?

Apart from the intrinsic quality of the product being demonstrated and the personal qualities of the demonstrator, the success or failure of a demonstration has much to do with the way in which it is approached by the prospective user. Even a small amount of preparatory work before a demonstration can save a lot of time on the day so that basic points of principle do not have to be laboured. Have the list of 'essentials' and 'desirables' to hand but do not produce it at the outset before the demonstration has got going or you will spend a lot of time talking and not very much seeing. If the product is not suitable it will become quite apparent during the course of the demonstration and you will have gained little by not seeing what the package *does* have to offer, even if it is merely to serve as a benchmark against which another product can be assessed.

If you wish to see specific reports or operations then it is only fair to warn the demonstrator beforehand so that he can set up some data to show these to their best effect. Do not expect the demonstrator to do copious amounts of work for you, however, and do not expect to see any amendments about which you are thinking, although it is surprising how often these are asked for before there is any firm commitment to purchase!

Remember that the intention of the demonstration, at least from your viewpoint, is to learn as much about the product in as short a space of time as possible and to assess the suitability of the system in your environment. It should not be a forum for scoring points off the demonstrator, nor for getting bogged down in long ideological arguments about whether the screen would look better in a different colour or whether you would like the balance to be shown at the top or the bottom of the customer statement.

Some people take great delight in posing difficult accounting questions to the demonstrator in the hope of catching him out. While you may feel this is necessary to gauge the level of expertise in the company, remember that if you know enough to have asked the questions in the first place, then you probably have little need to rely on the company other than for technical backup. Having said this, unless the demonstrator does understand the principles of accounting, the demonstration can be very hard work as you attempt to establish for example how, or even whether, accruals are reversed by the system.

Within reason, it is well worth attending demonstrations of a number of products. This will give you an invaluable basis for benchmarking (in its broadest sense) the products against each other and for assessing, at least informally, the quality of support and backup you can expect once on the road. A chaotic office with unanswered telephones ringing in the background should allow you to draw your own conclusions.

One important feature to note at the time of demonstration is the speed which is apparent in the system. You should establish on which machine the system is being demonstrated and, if this is different from your own actual or intended hardware, you should note that the speed of operation in your case may be slower. It is also worth remembering that demonstrations are normally carried out with files of limited sizes (say six customers, suppliers, nominal codes, etc). While this is perfectly adequate to put the system through its paces, it does mean that the time-consuming disk-bound operations are likely to be minimized and that the operation of the system with live data volumes may vary (adversely) considerably. At the end of the day, be very wary of a system which appears slow in a demonstration environment unless there is a very good reason which you can validate at the time.

Demonstrations of multi-user systems should allow for some time on the multiple access features of the package and you should make it clear before the demonstration that this should be the case. Some idea of the principles incorporated should be obvious from seeing what happens if an amendment to the same customer account (for example) is attempted simultaneously from two screens or if two users attempt to close a period at the same time.

WHAT TO DO WITH A SHORTLIST

At the end of the review of packages you will hopefully have arrived at a shortlist of acceptable products or, perhaps more depressingly, at the conclusion that you must pay for a product to be altered or start from scratch to meet your requirements. In many ways, the shorter the shortlist the better, as choosing between products which are similar in terms of price, facilities and position in the market can be hard, although most users by this stage have a 'gut feel' for the route they wish to pursue. If all other things appear equal, go for the route with which you would feel most comfortable in terms of ongoing dealings with the source of supply. Other factors which can sway otherwise marginal decisions are the ability of a system to cope with increased volumes and other software modules which are available from, or compatible with, the same source; you may not need them right now but you may do one day.

The advice generally given before finalizing a commitment to a specific product is to go and see one or more reference sites. While not gainsaying this as it has obvious advantages, not the least that it establishes that there is at least one satisfied user of the selected software, remember that you are unlikely to be pushed in the direction of a user who is going to be overtly critical of the system. Ideally, the reference site should be one which closely matches your proposed installation and this includes such factors as transaction volumes, number of users and patterns of processing. In addition to the applications software, the operating system and hardware may also need to be taken into account if these differ markedly from those with which you will be proceeding. It is now appropriate to take a closer look at these aspects.

OPERATING SYSTEM CONSIDERATIONS

While it is expedient to demote the hardware on which the system is to run to the bottom of the shopping list, the same cannot be said of the operating system. The operating system will dictate which applications will be available to you and, although it is possible to be dictated to in your choice of operating system by the applications software used, this would be unusual as there are normally wider implications to be considered.

The selection of an operating system is not to be taken lightly, although, for inexperienced users and those with limited ambitions, the ultimate effect of any particular choice may not be profound. For those users who will require to run other software and are alert as to the possibilities of in-house development and integration, the choice of operating system will be fundamental and will provide a constraining factor to the software, and even the hardware, which can be considered.

It may well be that your organization is already committed to a particular operating system environment and you will not be popular for bucking the trend. Even (or particularly) if this is your first or only venture into computing, you should still be aware of the operating system which is proposed, since getting too far out of the mainstream of the rest of the computer world may lead eventually to higher support costs and fewer options in adding to your systems or acquiring other software.

The disparity between operating systems is likely to assume less importance (at least in theory) as the concept of open systems permeates the business computer world but, nevertheless, it is still likely to retain its significance in the years to come.

HARDWARE CONSIDERATIONS

It is probably fair to say that many users effectively select accounting hardware rather than accounting software. This is almost invariably a mistake. True, you will need to know in broad terms the likely hardware and operating environment which you are likely to require. There is, for example, little point in spending time in looking at single-user systems if you know that you will require multiple access. There will also be cases, of course, where it is required to install an accounting system on existing equipment with a consequent restriction of choice.

As far as possible, however, be led by what you want the system to do, which means looking at the applications software which purports to do it. Only when you have this fixed (or at least a short list of viable options) should the hardware considerations come into play. If for no other reason, remember that in the fast moving world of the business microcomputer, the number of hardware options available is quite likely to have gone up between the start and end of a system selection process and, even more encouragingly, the cost of some of these options may have come down. Now there's an incentive to follow this advice!

When you do get to the stage of looking for accounting hardware, here are some of the points to bear in mind.

- Never mind the adverts in magazines or the salesperson's patter – choose hardware which is well known, well proven and well supported. Reliability is all; accounting systems are not the place to be pushing back the frontiers of technology.
- Try to get a feel for speed of performance, either through seeing a live system with similar volumes (best), looking at a demonstration (not as good) or working it out from published benchmarks (beware of jumping to conclusions!).
- Where multi-user software is concerned, get a feel for the operation by trying a few simple procedures on two stations concurrently, such as entry of invoice transactions or amendments to the same customer record.
- Think about other systems with which you may wish the accounting elements to relate; for example, graphical output (whether in display or printed form) will have implications on the hardware configuration selected.
- Remember that printers also constitute part of hardware and that many an otherwise good system has been brought to its knees by the use of a slow printer or one which is inherently unreliable or just 'difficult'. Again, reliability and simplicity are paramount and it is usually best to invest in the fastest printer within the constraints of your budget.

Never underestimate the amount of disk storage you require. Accounting systems have an insidious habit of gobbling up disk space and, as discussed in Chapter 4, you will need at least to provide for the following files:

- operating system program and utilities;
- accounting system program library;
- transaction files;

- □ master files;
- □ reference files;
- □ work files;
- □ index files.

This point about file sizes obviously dictates the hard disk storage capacity with which your system should be able to cope. It is unlikely that you will have specific knowledge of the size of all, or indeed any, of the individual files in the proposed system and you will normally need to be guided by the supplier or software house. As noted in Chapter 4, remember that the disk storage must be large enough to cope with the gradual increase in size inherent in master files (eg as new customers are added but old ones are not removed), increase in transaction volumes (as the business grows in activity), temporary files created during, say, end of period processing, and larger than normal file sizes when, for instance, the previous and current years are held open on the nominal ledger.

Some systems give good guidance as to how to calculate file sizes but, in reality, in these days when hard disk systems can come in hundreds of megabytes, even on microcomputers, the price of disk storage has now reduced to the stage that it is nearly always worthwhile obtaining the next higher increment of disk sizes available. If, for example, you think that you need a 40 megabyte (40Mb) drive then get a 80Mb model; if you think that you need 80Mb get a 120Mb drive and so on. In addition to securing greater safety in terms of free space, there is also likely to be a commensurate improvement in disk access speeds and this can have a marked effect on processing throughput, particularly on large ledgers.

6

Testing the System

THE NEED FOR TESTING

In the world of mainframe systems, it would be unthinkable that any critical application would be accepted for live running without a rigorous testing phase by the prospective users. In the more informal and immediate microcomputer environment, however, the need for such a process is often not recognized, either because the user has total confidence in the product, particularly in the context of a standard package with sales numbered in thousands or, it must be said, because the user lacks the experience necessary to appreciate what can go wrong. Such users may think that they will be able to abandon their old system (whether manual, mechanized or computerized) on one day and start the new system up on the next without so much as a break in service. Occasionally this may happen. A more pessimistic scenario would be that on Day One the new software is found to be incompatible with the hardware or operating system. On Day Two more gloom sets in as the users struggle to accommodate the existing ten character hierarchical nominal code within the six digit single level structure offered by the new system. By Day Three, when they realize that it will take nearly four days' worth of processing to close down the sales ledger each month they feel positively suicidal.

Even so, there may be some who would dispute the worth of system testing, even of a system which is as crucial as accounting, particularly where a standard (and unmodified) package is involved. Indeed, there is some sense in these arguments in the latter case as the principal virtue extolled in respect of such packages is that 'someone else has already found the bugs'. This assumes, however, that the sole purpose of testing a system is to look for software bugs. In reality, this is only part of the exercise, although where a bespoke or modified system is involved this will be a major consideration during the testing phase; however good the development work and testing by the software house, it is unlikely that every possible processing path has been tested and, more to the point, there is no better mainstream test of a system than a 'real user' using realistic data. Even proven products, however, will need some degree of testing to ensure that a smooth changeover can be achieved within an organization's specific mode of operation. Reasons for this include the following.

- An assertion that the main input and processing streams are fully understood and hence that the outputs from the system can be properly explained. In this way assurance can be gained about the way in which transactions will be processed in the live system and this in turn can be related to any special features of transactions (eg purchase ledger discounts or budgetary control procedures) which are specific to your organization.
- Following on from this, the opportunity to take the system quickly through its complete cycle of processing including period and year-ends. The latter is particularly important and is more difficult to test during pilot or parallel running. The year-end procedures on any accounting system are likely to contain some special provisions which do not apply at any other point in the accounting year, such as two years being open on the nominal ledger, the transfer of balances on profit and loss accounts to reserves or the need to reset budgets globally. As these procedures may not be encountered until 12 months or more after implementation, it is worthwhile establishing earlier rather than later the correct sequence and mode of operations.
- Printing a full set of reports from the system while the volumes are relatively small. By doing this, the reports can be filed as 'samples' and used to classify which should be mandatory, optional or not required in your system. This is far better than the waste of paper and time which can often result when 'seeing what this report looks like' once the system has grown to thousands of transactions and also prevents any potentially useful report from being overlooked.
- If there is any possibility of large value transactions or balances being processed or held by the system, now is the time to ensure that these are not going to cause any problems with data validations or numeric field overflows, either internally or on displays or reports. By the same token, you may wish to test the effects of a large volume of data, although this is a much more resource intensive exercise.
- In multi-user and network systems, the testing phase can be used to establish how the method of locking employed (assuming that there is one!) will affect your operational use of the system in terms of functionality and flexibility. This is particularly important as, besides considering how robust the system is, tasks will need to be scheduled so that, as far as possible, there is the minimum amount of conflict between users.
- The time taken for particular processes can be noted. If they take a long time with a small number of transactions in the system you can rest assured that they will take exponentially longer once volumes start to increase. Again, some knowledge of this is invaluable before designing your operating procedures.
- The controls inherent in the system can be established, thus enabling the manual controls which are to apply around the system to be defined.
- The input screens can be dumped to the printer for inclusion in operator instructions and can be used as a basis for the design of input forms.
- The data backup and restore operations can be developed and tested before any live data is involved.
- Most systems have some, hopefully minor, idiosyncrasies which may catch you by surprise; it is far better to be surprised in the privacy of a test rather

than hurriedly making up an explanation in front of a group of concerned and nervous staff.

- By the creation of a special set of test data (ie a test pack), subsequent modifications to the system can be more easily monitored and tested before acceptance into the live program library.
- The test area can also be used for the training of new users but it is worth preserving the original set of test data and restoring it after each period of training has been completed.

The above points illustrate that testing is by no means a trivial exercise, even in the most standard of systems. It is a chance for you to gain confidence in the new product and to see how it may be adapted to suit your own staffing and procedures. There will doubtless be features of the system which you may not want to use whereas there may be others which, not previously having realized their existence or potential, can be accommodated into your revised ways of working.

If time and enthusiasm permit it is worth compiling a test log document in which the tests carried out and their results can be noted. This brings some formality to the proceedings and, particularly, can be used to document problems, errors, anomalies or just plain bugs which are noted.

METHODS OF TESTING

Having established the need for testing, it is worth giving some thought as to how it is to be carried out. Many people confuse this stage of testing with parallel or pilot running. While it is true that these procedures, which are described in Chapter 8, form part of the overall testing and acceptance process, they are used as a forerunner to actual implementation, during which computer and manual processes can be refined in the light of experience of the live data encountered. They are not to be a forum for the testing of invalid or exceptional data (unless, that is, they happen to occur during the period of parallel or pilot running), nor are they for investigating the possibilities provided by the new system, again other than in terms of live data.

The degree and methods of testing will vary according to circumstances, depending upon such factors as:

- the amount of deviation from a known and proven standard package (in other words the perceived level of risk);
- the machine resources available;
- the time and labour resources available, not only for preparing and processing test data but also for checking the results.

In the event, therefore, testing may be as short as a day or as long as a piece of string, but it is worth bearing in mind that any problem, however minor, which is encountered after the testing stage will be more difficult to resolve than if it had been identified before the system contained any live data. On a more positive note, the more facilities which can be used at an early stage through testing, the more will be the benefit which is likely to be gained from the system from the outset.

The area used for testing may be one of the following.

- A separate area of hard disk (or even a different computer) from the live system. This has the advantage that the test area can be kept in place even once the system has been implemented; the disadvantage is that a separate loading of the program library may be required (with implications for disk space or even for licensing arrangements) which, in the course of time, may come to differ from the live program library.
- An initial implementation of the system which, after testing has been completed, will be overwritten when the system is reinstalled (or the files cleared down) for live running. This approach will not help with the testing of subsequent modifications or training but may be imposed by, for example, limitations of disk capacity.
- For systems which allow multi-company processing, it may be possible to set up a company purely for testing and training purposes. This will be good in terms of compatibility with the live system environment (as it will be the live system environment!), but will have implications in terms of disk space and, for some systems, the backup operation.

Whichever method is used, testing should not be viewed as a succession of *ad hoc* operations which happen to take your fancy while sitting at the screen and nkeyboard although, admittedly, even this is better than nothing. Rather, you should first sit down and draw up a set of objectives for your tests and decide how you will monitor the tests and determine whether they have been successful. In short, you will have to devise a test pack.

THE TEST PACK

Testing is often seen as a process of trying to find faults with a system. While this is to some extent true, it is a rather negative viewpoint and, if tests are constructed solely on the basis of trying to 'break' a system you will:

1. probably eventually succeed; and
2. probably not have learnt very much in the process!

There is, in fact, much more to be gained from testing, not least in terms of confidence and preparation for live running. While this is true for any type of application, it is particularly so for accounting where the penalties tend to be greater and the degree of dependence upon the system is total.

It has already been noted that the amount of resources which can be devoted to testing may be limited, and in any case circumstances will vary depending, for example, upon users' familiarity with computerized accounting systems and with the particular system under review.

Rather than approach the computer and start randomly to go through the menus, a more structured approach is to compile a test pack, ie a set of data which has been compiled for a specific testing purpose. A typical test pack is likely to include testing of such aspects as:

- normal processing;

- specific facilities or customized amendments;
- security and control;
- exceptional processing;
- high volumes (saturation testing);
- invalid occurrences.

The emphasis given to each type of test will vary. For example, saturation testing will not apply to small installations where the volume of transactions is likely to be low.

It is normally worthwhile keeping the different types of tests separate (although some intermixing is inevitable) as the tracing and resolution of problems tends to be easier in this way. Other than for saturation testing (in which high volumes and activity provide the whole point of the exercise), it is not usually necessary to use a massive amount of data; a perfectly good test pack can be provided by half a dozen customers and suppliers and a spread of nominal codes and cost centres. Add a few batches of transactions (say ten transactions per batch) and you will have the basis of a useful test pack.

Whatever you do, it is important to be aware of the basis of each test and to monitor (and preferably document) the actual results against those which are expected. In this way, you will build a set of data which can be used repeatedly in the future if and when amendments are subsequently made to the system.

TESTING OF NORMAL PROCESSING

The testing of the mainstream routes through a system with a set of 'typical' transactions will provide the bedrock of the test pack. The use of data modelled on your actual customers, suppliers and transactions is of great benefit as a good feel for how the system will cope with your actual coding, use of references, nominal analysis, etc can be gained. Although this is rather a late stage to find that, for example, the nominal code field will not accommodate your proposed coding structure (this being something which should have been established during the selection procedure), it is still better to know now than to find out later! A typical approach would be to use a few of your more active customers and suppliers as a base and to replicate some of their recent transactions. This type of testing should include at least:

- the initial system set-up, including the specification of any global parameters such as nominal codes for control accounts and any other 'system manager' functions;
- master file maintenance for customers, suppliers and nominal codes/cost centres;
- all principal transaction input streams including sales and purchase ledger invoice, credit note and cash entry and nominal journal and cash book inputs;
- ledger update routines;
- production of principal reports, ie ledger prints, list of customer/supplier balances, day books, journal listings and trial balance.

The above serves to prove the basic elements of the accounting system and should provide some confidence as to its method of operation and treatment of results.

TESTING OF SPECIFIC FACILITIES AND CUSTOMIZED AMENDMENTS

In addition to the principal routes through the system, there will be some facilities which will require special attention. These are likely to vary dependent upon the features provided by the system, the particular requirements of the user and whether there are any elements which have been programmed specifically to requirements. In general terms, however, such facilities are likely to include:

- period end processing on all three ledgers;
- year-end procedures;
- treatment of accruals;
- allocation facilities for matching sales/purchase ledger payments and credit notes against invoices;
- customer statement prints;
- supplier automated payment and cheque writing facilities;
- automatic journal facilities in the nominal ledger;
- supplementary reporting routines;
- VAT recording and reporting facilities;
- handling of information for budgetary control, including global revision of budgets;
- profit and loss and balance sheet definition and reporting facilities;
- use of report writer, spreadsheet interface or any other user definable facility;
- multi-user operation;
- any features which have been specifically programmed for your installation.

While you may think it worthwhile testing only those facilities which you are likely to use, remember that the testing phase provides an ideal opportunity to 'play' with any part of the system without worrying about the effects of your actions. Unless time is really pressing, using this opportunity to make a perusal of all the options provided may subsequently prove to be of great benefit, particularly in the light of the changing nature of business information requirements.

Particular attention should be paid to the last item in the list above, the features which are specific to your system. By definition, these are likely to be the weakest parts and, presumably, among the most important to you (otherwise why would you have asked for the amendments?). Naturally, the amount of testing will depend upon the scope and importance of the change in terms of the rest of the system, but be sure to use this period for ensuring not only that the changes work but that they are what you asked for. Again, finding out now, in advance of any live implementation and before your operating staff become involved, can save massive disruption at a later stage.

As noted previously, users with multi-user or networked systems will wish to spend some time in testing the operation of the record and/or file level protections offered during processing. This is a task which is particularly important before live work commences as problems may be attributable to operating system or hardware considerations rather than the applications software. Whatever the problems, there is little point in going ahead until they are resolved. Among specific points to look for are the effects of:

- two users making the same type of transaction input at the same time;
- two users attempting to amend the same master file record at the same time;
- general random usage of the system by two or more users; note when the processing of any one of them directly impacts upon the others;
- entry of a new master file record at one terminal which is then immediately accessed by a user making transaction input at another terminal;
- two users attempting an update of the same ledger at the same time;
- two users attempting to close the period on the same ledger at the same time;
- two or more users printing long reports at the same time.

In carrying out these operations do keep in mind the patterns of multi-user processing which you envisage and ensure that you have some sessions testing the system in these modes with the maximum projected number of users on line.

SECURITY AND CONTROL

Before taking the system into live running you will wish to understand, and be satisfied with, the controls applied by the system and the arrangements which need to be made for security. These subjects are dealt with in greater detail in Chapter 12, but among the aspects to watch for are:

- any user identification and/or password protection facilities, how they work and who can do what with a particular level of password;
- testing of the arrangements for archiving and, equally important, for restoring from an archive;
- the method of operation of any log which is operated by the system, particularly in a multi-user environment;
- operation of batch control facilities, including the options given in the event of a batch control failure;
- reconciliation of purchase and sales ledger control account totals with their respective balance listings and complete ledger listings and also with the corresponding control accounts in the nominal ledger;
- controls over input of balanced journals to the nominal ledger;
- review of trial balance and nominal ledger listing to ensure that the nominal ledger is in balance;
- operation of any utilities provided with the system, for example for checking the integrity of data files.

In general, in this element of testing, you should be particularly alert to the control functions of the system and ensure that you understand those controls which are applied automatically. Equally, consideration of other controls not provided by the system will assist in drawing up your own operational procedures.

The advice about testing archiving and restoration arrangements is also particularly valid. While most users get used to taking an archive copy of their data, very few bother to test that they are able subsequently to restore from it successfully. This is an ideal opportunity to test your understanding of the archive and restore operations and, even more importantly, to establish that they actually work! There are also other considerations: in a multi-company environment, for example, are you able to restore the files for one company without affecting the others? Finding out the truth at a later stage can sometimes be very uncomfortable!

EXCEPTIONAL PROCESSING

The satisfactory completion of testing thus far should give a high degree of assurance about the system's suitability to process your accounts. You can now move on to submit some of the more exceptional items into your test pack, not only to see that they are processed correctly but, of equal importance, to establish precisely how they are to be accommodated. Such items may include:

- write-offs of balances in the sales/purchase ledgers (such as the write-off of bad debts from the sales ledger);
- purchase or sales invoices with an abnormally high number of nominal code analysis lines;
- nominal ledger journals with a large number of lines;
- contra entries between supplier and customer accounts;
- 'unallocation' of allocated transactions;
- cheques which bounce (either yours or theirs!);
- payments or receipts 'on account';
- cash payments made to customers (eg in the case of a refund);
- similarly, cash receipts from suppliers;
- partial allocation of payments against invoices (if permitted);
- discounts disallowed;
- adjustment transactions, eg to reverse out an invoice posted to the sales ledger in error;
- entry of opening balances.

This element of testing is as much for your own benefit as a test of the system itself. All the above events can occur in any business and the methods found to accommodate their processing can usefully be included in your own operational procedures manual.

HIGH VOLUMES (SATURATION TESTING)

The testing of the effect of high volumes on a system is not necessarily applicable for everyone but, if you are likely to have a large processing requirement, it is worth spending more time in adding a volume test to your test pack.

In volume testing, not only will you be interested in knowing that the system will cope with the large throughput, but also in the degradation in processing and response times which might result, particularly in a multi-user environment. All systems will have internal limitations of some sort dictating the maximum number of records within a file (eg transactions in a a ledger) and so on. Hopefully, you would be unlikely to encounter these limits (which, in current systems, are likely to be far larger than any normal requirements), but you may instead run into problems with spare disk capacity or with internal fields or variables which may overflow when large values are encountered. As a trivial example, it is not unknown for the page numbering variable in reports to be held as a single byte with, therefore, a maximum value of 256 (ie 2 to the power 8, in practice page number 255 would be the highest printed as the lowest number is 0 and not 1) and hence pages above this value would not be numbered.

I am not suggesting that you devise sufficient data to test a report of this length, but you may wish to get a feel as to how the system copes under pressure. This applies particularly to multi-user or networked systems where the effects of more than one user can also be tested working 'flat out' at, say, transaction entry. This will be useful not only in ascertaining the likely effect on performance, but also in establishing the level of multiple access permitted by the file and/or record locking facilities incorporated in the software.

INVALID OCCURRENCES

This is the part of testing which can be the most entertaining although, in honesty, if the system under review is anything less than robust and if your other tests have been adequate, then you will already have found many of its frailties. Nevertheless, there is still some point in trying to test some 'impossible' events so that you can be on guard for any potential weaknesses in the system and, in extremis, you may wish to reject it or at least postpone further steps towards implementation until corrections have been made. 'Impossible' events can be triggered off in real life by operator error (eg neglecting to enter a decimal point to separate pounds from pence in the entry of a value which is in any case high), or by a physical event corrupting a field within a file.

This is one area in which a vivid imagination can be a great help but among the types of test you may wish to include are:

- entry of zero value or high value transactions (test both debits and credits separately for the latter as you may find that the maximum permitted values may differ);
- forcing of high value balances (eg following a consolidation of transactions after a nominal period end);
- attempts at single-sided or imbalanced entries to a ledger, for example entry of a nominal ledger journal which does not balance;
- deletion of customers/suppliers/nominal codes which have transactions on the ledger;
- attempts to get the sales and purchase ledger control accounts on the nominal ledger to disagree with the individual ledger balances;
- update of any ledger more than once with the same source data;

- entry of invalid dates;
- attempted entry of invalid account numbers, nominal codes, VAT information, etc at various points in the system.

If you really want to be devious and you do not mind the inconvenience (and, admittedly, risk to hardware involved) you may wish to simulate the effects of a power cut occurring part of the way through an important process. It would be unrealistic to expect the system to recover automatically from such an event but a good system will warn of an abnormal exit and prevent the user from ploughing ahead, advising (or preferably forcing) restoration from an archived set of data.

WHAT TO DO IF YOU HIT PROBLEMS

It would be surprising if, after all the above tests, you failed to hit upon something which either did not work or, more likely, did not work in the way that you imagined it might. What you should do first is document as fully as possible what was being tested and the precise problem encountered. This should specifically include any error message which may appear, however obscure or unrelated it may seem to you, and the last normal processing message displayed on the screen. It is so much more useful, for example, to have something like:

Test No : 123 (high values)
System : Purchase ledger
Function : End of period routine (menu 7 option 3)
Last system message : Processing – Phase Five
Error message : Numeric overflow encountered
Effect : Transaction missing from brought forward ledger

rather than: 'there was some sort of problem during the end of period routine when high values were being processed'.

The action taken naturally depends upon the type of problem encountered. An event as major as, say, a ledger failing to balance for no apparent reason or transactions having 'gone missing' or being duplicated would probably set alarm bells ringing as to the underlying soundness of the software. More confidence could be anticipated, however, if it is found that, for example, there is a low limit to the number of transactions which could be contained in any one batch of input. Such a constraint could doubtless be worked around by reorganising work accordingly.

Having taken the trouble to document the problems found in testing, it is then worthwhile to review their likely effect upon your implementation. This exercise is best carried out at the completion of testing as the various problems can then be seen in the context of the overall system and, more often than not, experiences which are documented as 'problems' in the early stages of testing are subsequently found to be attributable to misunderstanding the sequence of operations required or general unfamiliarity with the system. The extent of the review exercise depends largely upon the degree of thoroughness you wish to devote to this task as you will have probably by now have developed a fairly well-refined opinion as to the acceptability of the product. The criteria used in assessing problems also tends to be subjective. Some users will tend to rant and rave if there is so much as a mis-spelling on the screen, whereas others are quite happy as long as no obvious error message appears (neither approach is recommended by the way!). The following four gradings, offered with the tongue partly in the cheek, provide an example of the type of assessment which could be made.

Grade A fault : Catastrophic

This one is easy. It means that you cannot proceed with this system under any circumstances. This may be because of an inherent major fault in the software which is unlikely to be corrected in a timely or satisfactory manner or there is a vital (at least to you) facility missing which cannot be incorporated. It may be as well to ask yourself how you had got this far without having ascertained that this facility did not exist.

Grade B fault : Fundamental

This stops short of being catastrophic but may be sufficient to delay or postpone implementation plans while resolution is sought. This may involve an amendment being made to the software or a rethinking (or compromise) with regard to your own requirements or methods of operation. Perhaps you needed ageing in weeks, rather than months, from the sales ledger or a variety of profit and loss account formats from the nominal.

Grade C fault : Not ideal, but can live with

While this sounds rather like how some married people view their partners, it actually means that the problem has been noted but it can be worked around or even avoided completely in live running. It may, for example, relate to a report which you will never use or a condition (eg a high value) which is very unlikely to occur in your processing. If all else was well, then you would still be likely to proceed with the implementation.

Grade D fault : Trivial

These are the obscure or inconsequential problems that you are no doubt delighted to have found, given the normal level of satisfaction involved in believing that you are the first person to have hit upon a particular fault, particularly as you can smugly assure yourself that it will have no effect on your plans. These faults may be in the category of a screen message failing to clear or the misalignment of a column in a report. If you are really lucky you may discover a problem of the '... if the customer's name begins with 'S' and it's the first of the month and you enter a credit note as the first transaction for that customer then the system won't accept it ...' variety. If that is the case, well done.

With packaged software, the chances of any changes being made in the short, or even medium, term are low so that problems which you regard as being Grade A or Grade B are likely to mean that you will look elsewhere. Having said that, it is difficult to imagine any reputable software house not responding to a substantiated 'catastrophic' problem (ie major bug) but whether you will have the time or inclination to wait around while it is resolved may be debatable.

The other categories of problems are likely to leave you with a 'feel' for whether or not to proceed, probably dependent upon the number and type of problems experienced, the pressures to get on with implementation, your willingness to start again with another system and your natural level of optimism. If you feel so disposed, it may well be worth telling the dealer or the software house of the problems you have encountered. For a start it will be interesting to gauge their reaction (indifference not being a good start), but also you may be genuinely helpful in pointing out a problem which they may not have known about.

IMPLEMENTATION

7

Before the Changeover

THINK BEFORE YOU SINK

In the rush to get on with a new system, which is sometimes exacerbated by an old system that has ground to an ungraceful halt, it is often conveniently forgotten that there are a number of fundamental matters which should be addressed before live processing can commence. Some of these relate to documentation, others to security arrangements and yet others to staff involvement, training and responsibilities. While it is perfectly possible to go ahead without thinking about any of these aspects, and no doubt successfully so in a very small organization where the whole of the accounts operation is perhaps managed by one person, it can undoubtedly be a dangerous path to tread. Even in the case of the small organization, what would happen if that one person became sick or left the company?

Although it is relatively rarely seen in practice, the implementation of a new accounting system presents a chance metaphorically to draw one's breath, take stock and decide precisely how the running of *this* system will be so much better than the previous one. In practice, of course, things are rarely so simple and the mad dash to get opening balances in by the end of the week often subsumes all other thoughts. Nevertheless, if it is at all possible it is worth dwelling on some of the peripheral activities which go towards a successful implementation. If they are not thought about at the start, they are unlikely to be thought about at all.

DOCUMENTATION

A section on documentation may not sound the most riveting of opportunities but much of the success of operation of an accounting system is dependent as much on the quality of documentation which is used around it as on the standard of reporting by the system itself. Documentation does not merely relate to the manual which will accompany the software, although this is undoubtedly one of the more important items to have by your side, particularly in the early days of operation. In fact, there is much in the way of documentation which can be created by the user to make the system more effective for his specific environment. Such documentation will include:

- input forms;
- batch control registers;
- supplementary accounting records, particularly the cash book;
- operating instructions specific to your installation;
- backup register;
- fault log.

Each of these will be covered in the following paragraphs although there is, of course, no 'right answer' as to how (or even whether) each document is maintained in all organizations. There is little point in keeping documentation for the sake of it, but the tendency of some to think that pen need never be put to paper again after a computer arrives occasionally means that documentation can be somewhat under-represented in some installations!

Manuals

There was a time when the recipient of a microcomputer based accounting system would have been lucky to have had a few sheets of photocopied paper stapled together for a manual, but those days are long gone. The current purchaser of any well-known package is now far more likely to receive a thick and glossy ring-bound tome in a substantial presentation box, complete with cellophane wrapping. As well as the main part of the manual there are also likely to be tutorial guides and quick reference cards, not to mention the master diskettes for the package itself and for any on-disk tutorials which are supplied. There is little doubt that packaging and presentation have improved immensely over the years as have, in fairness, the quality of the products to which they relate.

While there is no doubt some advantage to be gained by reading the manual from cover to cover at some stage this need not necessarily be done at the outset. Indeed, the finer points of detail of operation are probably best left until a better global understanding of the system has evolved and some practical experience gained. What does need to be grasped at an early stage (and this means *before* implementation!) are the overall concepts of operation and, if you are on your own in this, the installation procedures. Most manuals have 'overview' chapters which are easy to peruse and a step-by-step guide to transfer of the software from the diskettes in the box on to your hard disk system.

However good the manual, you will quickly come to realise that it is not a substitute for the detailed definition of your own procedures. The manual will relate to the specific operation of the system, eg the fields which are available when a purchase invoice is entered or, in system terms, the routine to be followed for closing down a period. It will not, however, know how *you* want specific invoices to be treated or precisely what checks and reconciliations you will want to perform around the time of the period end. Hence, the software manual should be seen as part (and, admittedly, an essential part) of the system documentation but not, as is so often the case, the *only* part.

Input forms

Anyone who has used a mainframe accounting system will be used to the idea of formal input forms being used as the basis of entry of data, but their acceptance into the microcomputer world has been far less marked. Obviously, there are often major differences between mainframe and microcomputer scales and scopes of operations and there is little point in suggesting that a one-man business should take the time to devise and write out input forms for each transaction and master file record keyed into the system. Nevertheless there are advantages to be gained from the use of input forms, which include the following.

- The complete set of data relating to the transaction or master file record is defined *before* approaching the computer so that there is no reason to have to 'guess' at how fields should be entered when the input is actually made nor be 'surprised' when a particular item of data does not fit within the number of characters defined for that field. In this way potential problems over input are tackled away from the keyboard, where expediency, rather than accuracy, may dominate the operator's thinking.
- For master file records (ie customers, suppliers and nominal codes) an input form provides a documentary record of what was supposed to have been entered, this being particularly important for memorandum fields which may not be obvious from any other document. Not only that, the input form can have space for an authorizing signature, so that the presence (or subsequent amendment or deletion) of any master file record without this proven authorization can be questioned.
- Where the staff used for input are unskilled or subject to a high turnover, input forms provide a means by which consistency and accuracy of input can be controlled and the need for discretion to be applied while at the keyboard is removed.
- Input forms have the advantage of allowing data to be presented for input in the precise order required by the system being operated.
- Input forms provide an element of self-documentation and, for transactions, can be clipped to the source document in the filing system. Input forms for master file records can be filed in account code sequence so that a complete history for each account can be easily established.

Input forms are not all good news of course and, as well as the time and costs involved in their design and printing, they obviously add an extra overhead to the operation of a system although many think that this is more than repaid by the improvement in control and accuracy which results. Undoubtedly their use should not be introduced unless the scale of the operation merits it and, even then, you must be wholly committed to the success of their operation.

Perhaps the best example of the worth of input forms is in the case of purchase invoices. As anyone with purchase ledger experience will know, the quest for standardization has yet to make a marked impact on the world of invoices. Hence, a batch of such transactions invariably comprises a multi-sized and shaped bundle of papers, each of which has the information you will require to input in different places. Not only that, the analysis for nominal coding will need to be written somewhere on the document together with the supplier account number. By stapling an input form to the invoice this information can at least be read consistently from one invoice to another and any such contribution to such uniformity can be a great help.

Overall, input forms help to bring a measure of orderliness to an accounting system and remove the need to do anything other than key while at the keyboard. It is refreshing to note that many packages now include templates for input forms within their documentation, leaving the user merely with the task of photocopying in order to get going. An example of a typical input form, for the entry of nominal journals, is shown in Figure 7.1 and it should not be difficult to devise such documents for the various elements of the system which you are running.

Batch control register

The batch control register, as the name implies, provides for a convenient means of documenting and controlling the entry of batches of transactions into the system. The concept of batch control is discussed in Chapter 12 and is fundamental to the integrity of value-related transactions.

The batch control register should show the following types of details:

- ☐ batch number (normally a sequential number allocated by the system or by the user);
- ☐ type of batch (eg invoice, credit note, cash);
- ☐ date of entry;
- ☐ time of entry;
- ☐ batch total (calculated manually prior to input);
- ☐ batch total (calculated by system on input);
- ☐ cause of discrepancy (if the two totals do not match);
- ☐ action taken (in the event of a discrepancy);
- ☐ operator initials (ie the person who actually entered the batch);
- ☐ Supervisor initials (ie the person responsible for checking the output).

As noted, the numbering of batches is often effected automatically by the system with sequential numbering within ledger being one of the most frequently encountered principles adopted. A separate batch control register (or at least separate section of the same register) can then be used for each ledger and a similar numbering concept can usefully be adopted if batches are to be numbered manually.

As each transaction should have its batch number written on it, the register provides an easy means of establishing precisely when (or even if) that transaction was actually entered into the system. As an added bonus, because of its chronological nature, the use of the date and time columns can be invaluable if it is necessary to restore from a backup copy of data at some stage; processing can then be easily resumed from the first batch entered after the time and date of the backup from which the restoration was made. As a further advantage, the batch listings produced as the result of the original input may be sufficient to form the basis of the reinput of the transactions.

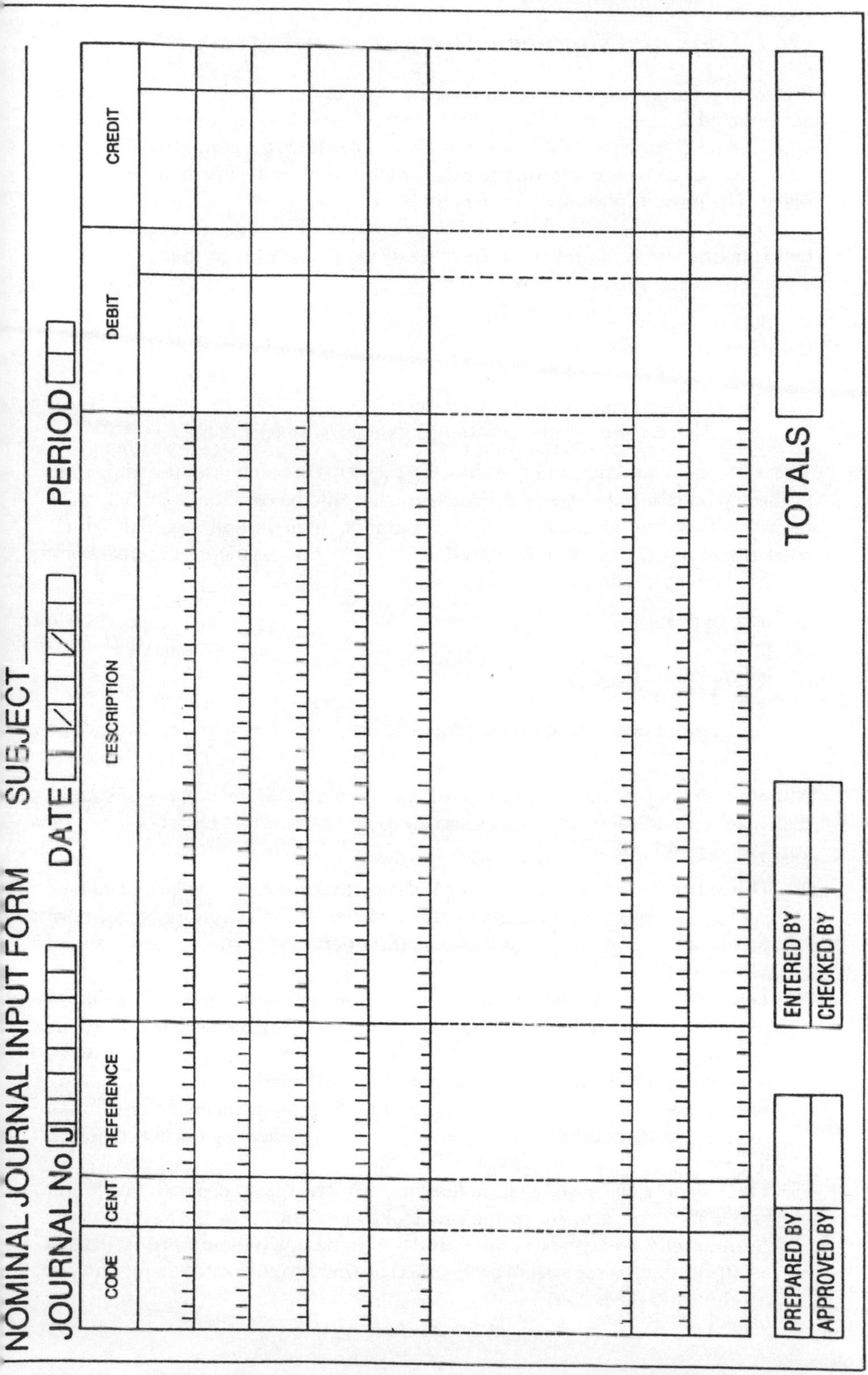

NOMINAL JOURNAL INPUT FORM SUBJECT ____________

JOURNAL No J

DATE __/__/__ PERIOD

CODE	CENT	REFERENCE	DESCRIPTION	DEBIT	CREDIT

PREPARED BY	
APPROVED BY	

ENTERED BY	
CHECKED BY	

TOTALS

Figure 7.1 Typical input form for nominal journals

Cash book and supplementary accounting records

It is a surprisingly common belief that the days of manual accounting records are finished forever once a computerized system has been installed. While this is by and large the case (otherwise why would you have the computer system?), there are still some accounting records which it is at least expedient to keep in place. The most important of these is the cash book.

The cash book provides for the initial recording of cheques (and other bank instruments) received and paid. In a 'traditional' cash book, there would be recorded for receipts:

- date received;
- from whom received;
- value;
- sub-total of receipts banked together;
- analysis of receipt, eg into payment by debtors, sales income or VAT.

The sub-total would normally be shown for groups of receipts on the same date as these would be paid into the bank as one deposit, the resultant total being the figure which would appear on the bank statement and against which subsequent reconciliation would need to be made. For payments, the cash book would show as a minimum:

- date of receipt;
- payee;
- cheque number;
- value
- analysis of payment, eg into payment of creditors, heads of expenditure or VAT.

Although it may sound Luddite to those who feel that computers should dispense with all manual tasks, this principle of retaining a cash book can be supported as follows:

- The only other ready source record of receipts and payments are primarily paying-in books and cheque stubs. These would be a poor form of permanent record and, in any case, could not provide an acceptable form of accounting record.
- The cash book provides an easily accessible and managed form of recording from which the continuity of transactions can be easily monitored.
- Cash items are likely to be entered into different modules of the accounting system, hence they do not always appear in chronological order in the bank (or cash book control) account which is maintained within the nominal ledger.
- There is only one cash book (at least for any one bank account), hence you know that you are, by definition, looking at the most up-to-date copy. Additionally, you can be assured that the cash book will be more, or at least as, up-to-date as the system as it is used as the source document for entry of receipts and payments.

- In practical terms, while the cash book should mirror the bank account held in the nominal ledger, reconciliation with the bank statement is made much easier from the cash book. One of the reasons for this is the bundling of receipts on paying in to the bank; the bundled sub-total would not necessarily be keyed in to a ledger system as it is the detail of the individual receipts which is of interest.

With operational sales and purchase ledgers, the analysis of receipts and payments needs to be little more than the ledger to which they are to be posted. As the items are entered to the system the account number or nominal code(s) can be marked at their side. For example:

Date	Payee	Chq No	Value	P/L	A/c	N/L	A/c
23 Dec xx	A Aardvark	123456	117.50	117.50	A53		
23 Dec xx	Council	457	2,000.00			2,000.00	105
24 Dec xx	B Beaver	458	235.00	235.00	B66		

Alternatively, if space permits, the nominal analysis headings can be listed across the page in conventional format.

In addition to the cash book there will also be other documents or books which you may wish to retain. For example, a purchase invoice register, detailing purchase invoices as they are received into the organization and where and to whom they have been sent for approval, is commonly found in offices where there is no equivalent computerized alternative within the purchase ledger. Similarly, a petty cash book is also frequently retained for the analysis and control of incidental cash expenditure. The underlying point is that, even though the accounting system will be computerized, there will nevertheless be a continuing need for some manual records to be maintained and these should be incorporated smoothly into the overall accounting office procedures.

Operating procedures manual

As noted earlier in this chapter, however good the manual supplied with the system, there will always be a need to supplement this with a definition of procedures specific to your organization. These may, for example, involve the definition of:

- an accounts processing timetable (see Chapter 11);
- instructions to cover end of period (and year) procedures on each of the ledgers;
- instructions relating to data backup and security;
- system controls and reconciliations which are to be applied;.
- instructions relating to any part of the system which has been modified to your requirements (and hence would not be covered in the standard product manual);

- details of how any unusual transactions which are specific to the organization are to be dealt with (in a multi-currency ledger for example, the rules governing the exchange rates used will need to be defined);
- specific hardware instructions relating to the accounting systems, eg routines used to change printers or printer pitch for particular reports.

The areas covered by such instructions and the degree of detail will obviously vary between installations but the principle of producing your own operating procedures manual should be noted and the document should be updated from time to time as new or revised instructions are issued.

Operating procedures need not necessarily be confined to accounts department staff. The introduction of a new system is often a good time to advise the rest of the organization of the changes in store and this can be turned into a good public relations exercise, particularly if you are able to demonstrate some benefits for those in other departments, such as improved provision of information for them or, on a more altruistic note, a faster turnround of staff expense claims. As part of this exercise there are likely to be some instructions which you would wish staff in other departments to receive and obey and, providing that the office politics and protocols are properly observed, it is as well to get these sent out before the system is operational so that any discord can be smoothed over before it really matters.

The operating procedures manual is also a sensible place in which to record the details of the specific hardware and software configuration (eg product names, specific version numbers, serial numbers, etc) and the contact and registration details for hardware, software and dealer personnel. Suppliers of consumables and stationery (including any special stationery used for the printing of customer statements, supplier remittance advice notes, etc) can also be usefully noted.

Backup register

As many have found to their credit (or cost), the backup register is one of the most vital documents relating to an accounting system or, for that matter, to any other system of importance. The backup register is simply used to record the time and date at which backup copies (or archives) of data are made. The concept of archiving is considered further in Chapter 10 but, in essence, the register is maintained to enable two questions to be answered:

1. If I need to restore from backup, which tape(s) or disk(s) should I use?
2. What state will the system then be in?

The backup register records, therefore, the following types of information in respect of each backup copy taken:

- date;
- time;
- operator;
- backup cycle letter;
- scope of backup (eg complete disk, specified directories or files);

- ☐ type of backup (eg daily, month end, *ad hoc*);
- ☐ number of tapes or disks used;
- ☐ identification (ie labelling) of tapes or disks used;
- ☐ last significant event before backup (eg last batch number entered);
- ☐ any comments about unusual events or messages, etc.

The inclusion of the time, as well as the date, enables the point in the day to be positively identified which if, for example, it is matched against the times recorded in the batch control register may help to pinpoint the place at which recovery work is to recommence.

As with any document of importance, the backup register should be reviewed periodically and the most recent entries checked against the backup media present in the office. Any slackness or discrepancies found should be viewed with concern as, in the event of a disaster, this register should provide the principal route to recovery. Staff should be aware of the importance of the operation (including the making of a correct entry in the backup register) and it should be one person's defined responsibility to ensure that the proper procedures are followed.

While on the subject of backups, remember also to take an occasional copy of the live program library (which, in the course of time, ie after various upgrades and revisions, may come to differ from the original system which was released) and also of any other peripheral files surrounding the system such as special user menus or configured command files. These files may, of course, be in any case copied by routine backups, particularly where a tape backup system is installed, but, if they are not, then this can save a great deal of time and effort in the gloomy event of your hard disk needing reformatting or replacing. Needless to say, the taking of such *ad hoc* copies of non-data files should also be recorded in the backup register.

Fault log

However optimistic you may be by nature, any computerized system experiences faults from time to time and there is no reason to assume that yours will be immune, although you can do much to help your own cause by careful management and good controls. Problems can arise from a number of areas, including:

- ☐ operator error;
- ☐ hardware fault;
- ☐ applications software fault (ie a bug);
- ☐ operating system problem;
- ☐ physical environment problem (eg power cut).

Not all problems are terminally serious but, particularly with an accounting application, you should always be alert to potential danger. For example, if you had a power cut during an end of period purge of a ledger then you are likely to have experienced some damage even if the system does not immediately report it. In such circumstances it can be folly to go on blithely as if nothing has happened as there is very little with which you can get away when the integrity of accounting data is at stake. You should always be ready to stop processing, print a few fundamental reports and run any checking utilities provided with the package before moving cautiously on or restoring from a backup copy.

At a time when many people are likely to lose their heads, the maintenance of a fault log can help you to retain yours and even to contribute some constructive comments based on past experience. The fault log would detail, for example:

- date of occurrence;
- time;
- brief description of fault;
- process being effected at the time that the fault occurred;
- last normal message displayed by system;
- any error message displayed;
- 'What happened next?';

Additionally, in multi-user and networked systems:

- which other machines and users were in operation at the time the fault occurred?
- what were they doing at that time?
- what effect, if any, did the fault have on their processing?

In this way any patterns in faults can be more quickly established, the underlying causes more realistically assessed and, in the long run, this will be likely to save support time and costs. It is not an answer to all the problems, but it is another example of managing the computer system in a disciplined and responsible way.

Filing

There is often a vague air of anticipation in the inexperienced that the introduction of a computerized system will reduce the amount of paper in an office. Indeed the 'paperless office' is often promulgated by the marketing of high-tech companies. In the early 1990s there is still some way to go to get to this state, at least in terms of accounting systems, although the advances made in various types of backup storage, particularly optical disks with their 'write once, read many times' (WORM) characteristics, and with electronic data interchange (EDI), may see things change during the course of the decade.

As they stand, however, accounting systems live and breathe on paper. The computer may provide you with the means to keep your accounts but the actual accounting records themselves and the supporting documentation will all need filing, preferably in a manner in which it is possible for them to be found again. The actual regime imposed varies from office to office, but thought will need to be given at least to the filing of the following documents:

- copies of sales invoices and credit notes;
- purchase invoices and credit notes;
- input forms for transaction entry;
- input forms for master file maintenance;
- batch input reports;

- ☐ 'mandatory' end of period reports, eg ledger listings, lists of balances, day books and journals;
- ☐ other reports, eg ageing analyses, management accounting reports, master file listings, user logs;
- ☐ supplier statements;
- ☐ copies of customer statements (if retained);
- ☐ other documentation and correspondence with customers and suppliers;
- ☐ other supporting documentation (eg schedules, support for journals).

The use of proper printout binders, which can be labelled, for holding reports should be more or less compulsory with any reasonable volume of data. The various items of ancillary office furniture designed to facilitate the storage of and access to such binders are also a good investment. Filing takes time and this is a fact that should be recognized in staffing and operational plans. In an accounting environment (as, for that matter, in many others) poor filing can waste hours at a later stage and, conceivably, could even result in a more direct financial loss. Staff need, therefore, to recognize the importance of what is likely to seem a mundane and unexciting task and if the most frequent phrase heard in your office is something like 'we can't find the invoice', it is time that some attention was paid to it. Depending upon storage space available to you consideration will also need to be given as to where old (say before the previous financial year) papers are held.

Rubber stamps

We are getting somewhat into the realm of general office procedures, but there is little doubt that accounting systems run better with the judicious use of rubber stamps. A simple example is the use of such stamps for purchase invoices which will need to be marked in various ways in their journey through the system, with such events as:

- ☐ date received;
- ☐ internal reference number;
- ☐ purchase order number;
- ☐ goods received note (GRN) number(s);
- ☐ acceptance (ie approved for posting) box (and approver's initials);
- ☐ posted (to the purchase ledger) box (eg with batch number);
- ☐ paid box (eg with cheque number).

It should be possible to pick up any purchase invoice in the organization and, without reference to anything else, correctly deduce its present status. For example, has it been posted to the ledger? Has it been paid? If you do not know the answer to these questions what will prevent you from posting it twice or, even worse, from paying it twice? Do not think it cannot happen because the 'paid' invoices happen to be filed separately. One day someone will remove an invoice from the file and accidentally return it to the wrong file or leave it in the in-tray of purchase invoices waiting to be batched for entry to the system. Think where and how you will want to use rubber stamps or any other marker for the source documents within your system.

STAFF

It is fair to say that there are now relatively few companies which have not had at least a passing acquaintance with a computer system, even if that acquaintance was not of a particularly friendly nature. Hence, it is now less likely that the words 'They're going to get a computer' will strike abject fear into the staff involved than once it might have done, depending of course upon any previous experiences they may have had!

Most staff involved with the maintenance of accounts at any level will by now come to expect some involvement with computers and, for many, this is welcomed as an interesting, even prestigious, enhancement to what in the past may have seemed a rather unattractive or unglamorous job. In theory at least, the automation of routine, and labour-intensive, tasks such as the transcription of entries between the various accounting records or the casting of ledgers allows expansion of duties to other matters which would once have been beyond their remit. Hence, accounting staff may become involved in the analysis of information or the use of associated systems such as spreadsheets or presentation graphics. Unfortunately, however, the increase in transaction volumes which often follows hot on the heels of the implementation of an accounting system frequently means that the existing staff become subsumed in the deluge of input required merely to keep up to date as there is a natural reluctance by management to point at an increased level of staffing following the system's introduction.

In an ideal environment, accounting system duties would be spread among staff sufficiently to ensure that there is an adequate division of responsibilities from a control viewpoint. In many organizations this is simply not possible as there are more responsibilities than there are staff and, as noted above, there are few who would be brave (or should it be reckless?) enough to ask for more staff at this stage. Even so, the point should not be lost. If one person can, for example, set up suppliers, enter purchase invoices and control payment runs, and do all of this with minimal supervision, then there must be some risk involved.

As almost any book on computerization will tell you, staff should be involved from an early stage of a new project or, if not involved, then at least kept informed. This is not a placebo merely to be acknowledged but, particularly if you are transferring from one computer system to another, the advice of the staff who carry out the day-to-day operations on the old system can be invaluable, not least in giving pointers as to what should be avoided when selecting a replacement system. It is however unfortunate, but all too often true, that their opinion of the existing system will sometimes be so unfavourable that they will view almost any possible replacement in a more positive light!

A new system will normally herald revised procedures, new coding conventions, different controls and so on and there may well be a traumatic period to be experienced as one system is traded for another. Apart from any turmoil that may be caused internally, think also of how your organization will appear to external eyes, ie those of your suppliers and, more importantly, customers. They may well take a dim view if they are dealt with inefficiently and, in extreme cases, may even take their future business elsewhere. Much of their perception will depend upon how your staff deal with queries and problems and it will be virtually impossible to succeed without their active (and that means constructive) co-operation. The more that you can pave the way for this sort of assistance the better.

Training

As with most new ventures, the level of training required is largely dependent upon the aptitude and level of staff employed and the degree of dissimilarity of the new system from its predecessor. This dissimilarity is not merely related to the accounting software, however, as changes to hardware and/or operating systems may also uncover gaps in expertise which may usefully be filled by some introductory training in these elements. The company from which the system is acquired is obviously a good place to turn as your first resort; indeed some companies will include an element of training and 'hand holding' in 'getting going' within the purchase price and more would usually be available on a commercial basis.

On a more general front there are a large number of specific training organizations offering introductory courses on the more popular hardware, operating systems and, occasionally, accounting software. With regard to the latter, the software houses behind the products may well hold courses of their own and you should receive details of these types of services when you register as a user. If the software has been acquired on the advice of an auditor or consultant then they may be another port of call for guidance and assistance.

If at all possible, allow your staff to familiarize themselves with the system at their own pace and, in this respect, much can be achieved through the use of a 'training company' (perhaps as part of a multi-company set-up) or a separate tutorial installation of the system in another part of the disk. This imparts the confidence that they can make mistakes without having any adverse effect on live data and allows them to test the effect of a particular action before committing themselves to it. As another aid to familiarization, many well-known packages now come complete with on disk tutorials and this provides another useful tool to help you along the way.

Remember also to extend your thinking towards future changes in personnel. Many systems start to go awry when those with experience of the initial implementation and training leave and are replaced with staff with no detailed familiarity of procedures. It is here that the training facilities which you have created come into their own and will prove invaluable in getting the new recruits 'up to speed'.

The system manager

It is also useful to appoint, at least in principle, a member of the accounting staff with a suitable aptitude as the 'system manager' for the new installation. This person should have the responsibility for the general day-to-day operation of the computerized element of the system and, among the doubtless many duties which can be invented for him are the following.

- Basic system maintenance and troubleshooting. This implies a degree of familiarity with the hardware and software and simple operating system tasks such as copying files between hard and floppy disks and determining the available free space on a hard disk drive.
- Responsibility for archiving arrangements. This does not necessarily mean that the system manager has physically to effect each backup, but it does imply maintenance of the backup register and the responsibility for ensuring that backup media is supplied, labelled and stored in accordance with the defined procedures. 'Responsibility' really does mean just that in this instance and the lucky person should be left in no doubt as to the importance of this task.
- In multi-user and network systems, give the system manager general control over resource utilization and task scheduling so that the conflicts between users (at least in computing terms!) are minimized. For example, two users simultaneously starting major disk-intensive tasks would themselves be disadvantaged and it would be downright disastrous for any other poor user of the system at that time. This is the sort of situation which can be avoided with a degree of planning and management.
- The system manager should liaise with external parties such as hardware suppliers, engineers, dealers or software houses. In all these cases, they will appreciate the single point of contact as it will generally cut down the time spent on support and, as a benefit to you, increase the knowledge of your system manager.

In some organizations, the system manager's role is effectively fulfilled by someone from another department, particularly where the organization is large enough to have its own MIS or IT support centre function. While this is certainly better than nothing, there is still something to be gained by using one of your own accounts staff for the task if possible. He or she will undoubtedly gain some invaluable systems experience through carrying out this role but, more importantly, will have a good understanding of problems in accounting terms, something which is often lacking in those from outside the accounting arena. For example, explaining to someone that your accruals have not reversed correctly is likely to be easier if you actually know what an accrual is.

Having just expounded the virtues of appointing a system manager, one should also cast a slight shadow over this advice by interposing a reminder about the security of the system. The system manager will, almost by definition, have access to the system not enjoyed by other users, which will be particularly true in networked or multi-user systems. He will enjoy privileges and functions which may not be available to 'normal' users and may also be able to have unsupervised sessions at the keyboard; in fact supervision may in any case be difficult if your own knowledge of computing lags behind. Remember, with an accounting system, *always* think of security and *always* be aware of control.

SUPPORT

The final element to get in place before commencing serious work on the new system is support. Those lucky enough to have internal computing expertise available will be shielded from some of the problems which can afflict the users of accounting systems but, even so, there are still the following factors to consider.

Hardware maintenance

Only the most optimistic (or foolhardy?) of users will run a computerized accounting system without establishing a formal hardware maintenance agreement, particularly as reliance on manufacturer's warranty normally means a return to the factory without a replacement and, therefore, a potential time-lag until the machine reappears. When setting this up remember to check what service you are getting and for what equipment. A next-day response may not be quick enough if your system is used heavily for sales order processing and invoicing but, in a multi-user or network system, it may not be necessary to have the same level of cover for all the hardware elements. In a network, for example, the file server(s) will obviously need a high priority call-out but the same need not be true for all of the work stations as the temporary absence of just one may not prove too inconvenient. Whatever is selected, remember to include cover, or at least provide contingency, for the printer (or printers) used by the accounts system as the absence of this can be just as disruptive as the breakdown of the computer itself.

Software maintenance

Software maintenance is a far less tangible entity than that for hardware but a support contract is likely to be available to registered users of most leading packaged products. Such contracts are likely to include:

- telephone 'hot line' support;
- advice on reported bugs and anomalies;
- user newsletters;
- discounts on product upgrades;
- details and special offers on related products from the software company.

Some products have a compulsory maintenance contract which effectively becomes an annual licence fee. There is nothing wrong with this providing that it is made clear at the time of purchase. Where a formal software maintenance contract is optional, experienced users sometimes opt out and the decision is often a fine balance between cost and perceived worth and part of this equation is what happens if you do *not* take out such a contract. In general, inexperienced users and those with complex systems (either heavily amended or in a complex multi-user environment) would do particularly well to consider taking up a contract.

General operational support

In truth, many problems relating to accounting systems are of the day-to-day variety where it is advice on general problems which is required rather than an obvious hardware or software maintenance call. Indeed, for many users, it is not always obvious precisely which element of the system is malfunctioning; for example, a report containing gibberish could equally be caused by a corrupt data file as a faulty printer. Other requests for help may not relate to faults at all but to operator error (eg of the 'we have posted some invoices as credit notes by mistake' variety) or just plain guidance as to how to perform a particular function. The person(s) to whom you will turn in such times may have a significant effect upon the well-being of your system.

In essence, your support arrangements need to be clarified and in place *before* you are running the system in a live environment. Different users need different levels of support and, of course, the higher the level of support selected the higher will be the cost. In general, your reliance upon third parties will decrease with time as any hardware or software faults are ironed out and management and staff become familiar with the system. Even so, if and when disaster strikes it can be worthwhile having as many people on your side as possible – you may need them!

8

The Changeover

A TIME OF SEVERE STRESS

To say that the introduction of a new accounting system frequently heralds a time of severe stress in an organization is probably something of an understatement. Some companies barely recover from the disruption and delay that the new regime can bring. There is, of course, often a tendency to blame 'the computer' and the excuse of 'it's our new computer system' can work wonders for cash flow if suppliers who are asking for payment of their previous months' invoices believe it.

While it is certainly true that hardware, software or even operating system faults may manifest themselves during the early days of live running, just as they could at any time in the future, the problems surrounding implementation are more likely to reflect upon the quality of management rather than that of the system. Even in a perfect world, the introduction of any major change will have some unforeseen repercussions, but it is in the interests of all to try to minimize their incidence and effect. There are few worlds less perfect than that surrounding a new computer system and it is irresponsible to imagine that it can be implemented without some realistic thought being given to its introduction.

Those with experience of computerized systems will recognize the need for testing, training and defining procedures as activities which need to be carried out *before* reliance is placed on a system in a live situation. Never can this be more the case than with an accounting system and equally careful considera-tion needs to be given as to how the system is to be introduced, ie the changeover from the existing system whether it be manual or computerized.

It must also be appreciated that not everyone starts from the same point. In fact there are a number of positions on the 'starting grid', including the following.

- A new company with not even an existing manual system in operation. A really clean start; requires new hardware and new software but, unlike the others no strategy is needed for the transfer of existing accounts.

- □ An existing manual or mechanized system. Also requires new hardware and new software.
- □ An existing computerized system. Requires new software. May also require new hardware or an upgrade to existing hardware.
- □ An existing computerized system in which the hardware is to be replaced. This requires a change in hardware but may also necessitate a new version of the applications software being acquired.

The position on the starting grid matters not so much in terms of the direction to be taken so much as the route which must be followed to get to the journey's end. The first and last positions imply the easiest rides.

Remember that computerizing just to get yourself out of a mess can easily land you in a bigger one; the oft-quoted phrase 'to err is human but to really foul things up requires a computer' is not necessarily an idle jest!

HOW TO GET IT WRONG

As with many critical operations, it is easier to say how to get it wrong rather than how to get it right. The following hapless manager's 'fairy tale' illustrates a more or less guaranteed recipe for disaster. It is based upon events which I have seen or heard about on many occasions.

April 1 The start of a new financial year. Year-end accounts a long way from preparation on old ledger card system. Resolve to get computerized system for the new year's accounts.

May 1 Get round to visiting a couple of dealers and reading some magazines. Do not understand a word of what anyone says. Decide it is more difficult than you thought.

June 1 Year-end accounts still not completed. Getting desperate. Speak to business acquaintance in pub who is running a 'Supa' accounts package. Says it works without problems. Forgets to tell you that it has taken three years of consultancy fees to get to that state. Neither do you appreciate that his business is selling fish to cash customers and yours is manufacturing machine tools.

July 1 Buy 'Supa' package after shopping around for cheapest price. Delay for a week while you send it back as you have forgotten to specify that you need it on a 3.5in disk rather than on the 5.25in diskette on which it was supplied. Delay for another week while awaiting a memory upgrade for your computer to enable the program to load.

August 1 Get going at last. Set up all of the customers you have dealt with for the last five years on the customer file and similarly for supplier file. Find that you need some nominal codes in the system. Ring up accountant for advice. It is August. Your accountant is on holiday. Wait another two weeks.

September 1 Can get going at last. Too busy to test or prove the system so stop all processing on old system and start keying in transactions from 1 April, the start of your financial year. Autumn is your company's busiest time of year. Staff are stretched, as are your nerves.

October 1 Ten batches of April sales ledger cash receipts are entered as payments in error. Have been too busy to take a backup from the outset. Have choice of reversing and re-entering the payments or reinstalling the system from scratch. Choose the former but lose another two days. Two staff hand in their notice.

November 1 Various suppliers threatening litigation. Discover that you have failed to set a vital indicator to keep transactions open on the sales and purchase ledgers at period end so that all the April transactions have been consolidated into single balances. Annoying 'INTEGRITY FAILURE' message has started to appear on the nominal ledger and the trial balance doesn't (balance that is). Too busy to do anything about it.

December 1 Customers think it is Christmas, which it very nearly is. They have not received a statement for over three months and there is no credit control in operation.

January 1 With a massive amount of effort over the Christmas holidays, you are nearly up to date but, on the first day of the new year a 'DATE EXPIRED' message appears on starting up the system and you cannot get into the menus. Ring up supplier (remember, the one you got the best price from) – supplier no longer in business. Ring up 'Supa' headquarters. Closed for Christmas holidays. Wait a week and ring again. 'We do not talk to end users, you must go through your dealer'. Give up. Run rest of year with all transactions dated 31 December of previous year.

There will be few readers with experience of computing who will not recognize some truth in the above, although hopefully few will have travelled the whole sorry path. There is, of course, no need for such a bleak scenario, but the changeover to a new system is often stressful because of a lack of understanding of what is involved. This in turn results in some users doing too much, such as running two systems in parallel for far longer than they need, or too little, such as abandoning one system in favour of another without any thought of proving that a conversion has been correctly effected.

The three key elements to be considered are:

- the *timing* of the implementation;
- the *conversion* of data and proving integrity;
- the *method* of changeover.

Each of these elements may be tackled in a number of ways and there is no universal answer for all installations. Remember, as the manager who is masterminding the changeover, your prime objective will be to achieve a seamless conversion to the new system with the minimum of effort and disruption. Nothing more, nothing less. Decisions as to when and how the changeover will be effected should be made with this objective firmly in mind.

TIMING IMPLEMENTATION

There are three principal approaches to the take-on of data for a new system which can be conveniently classified as follows.

Retrospective

Keying in opening balances at some prior date (eg the start of the financial year) and then replicating all transactions from that date up to the present and beyond.

Current

Selecting a current date (eg the 1st of the next month) and keying in opening balances at that date and then transactions from that date.

Future

Selecting a current date (eg the 1st of the next month) and keying in to the new system only transactions relating to that date or beyond. All transactions before that date being continued to be processed by the old system. No opening position to be entered at outset although, of course, balances must eventually be transferred from the old system.

It must be said that, in an ideal world, all accounts systems would be implemented on the first day of a new financial year. All transactions for the whole of that year are then processed through the same system, giving advantages in terms of consistency, not only in terms of processing, but also in the presentation of reports. Note, however, that there will still be the need to key in outstanding sales and purchase ledger transactions and the opening balances (whenever they become available) to the nominal ledger. Hence, the level of work required is not necessarily markedly reduced by an implementation at this time.

The world is not ideal, however, and it should not be thought that the start of a financial year is the *only* time at which a system can be introduced. The year-end, by definition, tends to be a fraught time in many accounts offices and the teething problems of a new system may simply exacerbate the situation. The golden rule is to introduce a new system when both you and it are most ready and when the chances of successful implementation are at their highest. This may mean an introduction during the 'slack season' (assuming there is one), part of the way through the year. One thing is certain, an unsuccessful implementation can have near catastrophic consequences and you will be building on quicksand if things do not go well from the outset.

One of the most frequently posed questions about implementations part of the way through a financial year relates to whether the implementation should be attempted on the 'retrospective' basis. If, say, the year starts on 1 April and a system is introduced on 1 July, then should all the transactions occurring since 1 April be entered to the new system so that the effect at year-end will be to have a complete year's transactions within the one system? Like many questions that sound easy, there is no correspondingly easy answer. Obviously, much depends upon the volume of work required to be able to revert to a 'start of year' situation and the resources available to effect it; these factors will vary considerably between organizations.

The parameters in the equation to evaluate the answer to this include:

- the number of months (or other accounting periods) involved;
- the volume of transactions per month;
- the staff resources available for data entry and, just as importantly, checking against expected results;
- the amount of optimism felt that there will be no problems!

The answer is likely to be subjective to say the least. I tend to be against this form of retrospective implementation as it throws the maximum strain on a system when it has the maximum chance of going wrong, either through a system 'teething problem' (particularly for tailored or bespoke systems), or just because staff are unfamiliar with the basic routines and procedures. There is nothing more daunting or depressing than falling steadily behind with a system on which you are supposed to be catching up.

For this reason, the 'current' approach is sometimes preferable. The current date may, of course, coincide with the start of the new year but, whether it does or not, there is far less initial strain imposed on the system and, in dealing with current transactions, staff are likely to be better placed (and motivated) to resolve any problems. Fears of a lack of continuity part of the way through the financial year can be assuaged by retaining properly documented conversion reconciliations. There are, of course, some disadvantages and, for example, cumulative figures held on an annual basis (such as customer or supplier turnover figures) and period-by-period variances against budget may be more difficult to obtain on a consistent basis.

The 'future' approach is perhaps superficially attractive in that it removes most of the potential problems regarding data at the time of conversion. Indeed, there is no need even to prove the conversion by comparison of balances between the old and new systems and the bare minimum of customer and supplier accounts need to be set up, ie just those for whom transactions occur in the future. The bad news, however, is that, in effect, you will need to operate two sets of books (with no automatic interface or consolidation) until such time as the old system is finally closed down. Not only is this tedious in terms of the production of management accounts but also there is the danger of a transaction being posted to the wrong system if staff are not absolutely clear as to the correct procedures or, if things become particularly chaotic, being posted to both systems. Dealing with customer and supplier queries also becomes more difficult as there may be need to reference both systems and the possibility of customers receiving more than one statement from you may make this method prohibitive for a sales ledger.

DATA CONVERSION

Many of the considerations relating to changeover are connected with where you are coming from as much as where you are going to. For those with a manual accounts system for which this is the first computerization there will be no choice other than to set to work keying in master file details. For those converting from another computer system, however, the option may exist to transfer the data from the outgoing to the incoming system. This often sounds an attractive proposition and, indeed, it is if it is feasible. It may not always be so, however, and, while it may sometimes be difficult for the layman to understand, there are a number of factors which may work against it:

- The two systems may be on entirely different types of computer and running under different operating systems, making any direct conversion problematic without technical assistance to surmount the difficulties posed by the communications and data recording requirements.
- Even if the two systems are running in compatible environments, the file structures and formats will be markedly different. To effect a conversion successfully you will definitely need the active technical co-operation of the people behind the new system and, possibly, also those from the old system. There may be fields on your old files which have no equivalent in the new system and vice versa. The size and nature (in data format terms) of corresponding fields may also differ so that, for example, a special utility may be required to convert the nominal codes held by one system to a different structure in another.
- Although accounting systems are, in broad terms, similar, the detailed methods of processing will differ. Conversion of transaction data in particular may, therefore, be difficult because, say, the ancillary files used to hold information supporting the VAT return are processed under different principles in each of the two systems.

In effect, even if an automatic conversion is mooted, it may effectively need to be limited to the principal master files, ie customers, suppliers and nominal codes, although this is certainly better than nothing. There are, however, sometimes advantages in building up these files from scratch in the new system as:

- you will not have the costs associated with data conversion nor the risks of something going awry;
- your old system files may contain customer and supplier accounts which are dormant, ie there have been no transactions with them for quite some time, and there is little point in carrying these over into a new system;
- all data is positively entered into the new system in the correct format and any additional fields can be utilized.

Many people find the entry of opening balances into ledgers puzzling and, although many packages provide special facilities for this operation, it does need some thought. The techniques employed are discussed further in Chapter 9; suffice to say here that you should be very much on your guard against any transaction being 'double counted' in terms of the nominal ledger, eg an outstanding sales invoice appearing twice in the sales account, as a result of having been entered into both old and new systems.

PROVING THE CONVERSION

Unless the 'future' method of implementation is chosen (ie that in which no opening position is entered in the short term), wherever data comes from (even if it is keyed in from a manual system) there will be a need to prove that the initial files on the new system have been set up correctly, ie that the new system starts from a position which is reconcilable with that being discarded. This reconciliation may not merely relate to the ledgers, although the integrity of the transactions in the new system will be of primary concern, but also to the master files and other reference files held by the new system.

The degree of scrutiny given to the transition between the old and new systems will to some extent depend upon the volumes involved and the environment in which the system is operated. As an absolute minimum, however, the following figures should be checked between the new and old systems and the relevant printouts or documents initialled *and retained* as evidence of this:

- the balance of sales ledger control account (from within the sales ledger);
- the balance of the purchase ledger control account (from within the purchase ledger);
- the total of the list of customer balances;
- the total of the list of supplier balances;
- the number of customers;
- the number of suppliers;
- the debtors control account in the nominal ledger (which should also be equal to the control account in the sales ledger);
- the creditors control account in the nominal ledger (which should also be equal to the control account in the purchase ledger);
- nominal ledger cash account balance reconciled with the cash book.

The above represent the bare minimum. If time and/or resources permit, then a review of individual customer, supplier and nominal balances should be conducted to ensure that no compensating errors have crept in during the conversion processes and the customer and supplier master file details could be checked in more detail. There is absolutely no point in proceeding if the conversion cannot be demonstrably proved to have been successful.

Neither is there any point in making a conversion exercise any more difficult than it need be and those who are changing from one computer system to another can do much to help themselves. To this end, always effect a conversion at a point in time when there are no transactions which are awaiting posting to the ledger or, in invoicing systems, invoices or credit notes which have been entered but have not yet been printed and passed to the sales ledger. Having each of the ledgers fully posted minimizes the amount of data which needs to be converted and removes any confusion which might otherwise arise through having transactions entered in one system (and hence appearing on batch reports, etc) and being posted to the ledger in another. In reality, a conversion exercise would almost invariably be carried out at the end of a period with all three ledgers held at the same point in time.

METHODS OF IMPLEMENTATION

At some stage the method by which implementation is to be achieved will need to be decided. The traditional methods used are:

- *parallel running* in which the new system and the old are run side by side;
- *pilot running* in which the new system is run for part of the overall installation;
- *direct changeover* (sometimes known as 'big bang') in which the new system is introduced and the old one simultaneously abandoned.

The concept of each of these philosophies is well documented in books on systems analysis and design, but a quick briefing in the context of an accounting system is probably worthwhile. First, however, let us take a quick look at another variable in the conversion equation: phased implementation.

Phased implementation

Each of the above methods may be combined with another mechanism for introduction, the phased implementation, in which the new system is introduced in stages, perhaps nominal ledger initially, followed by purchase ledger and finally sales ledger. This method would be particularly applicable for integrated systems with a large number of modules (eg sales invoicing, sales order processing, stock control, purchase order processing, payroll, fixed assets) for which the prospect of 'going live' on all at once may be daunting. A phased implementation may proceed over a number of months, perhaps as follows:

- Phase 1 : nominal ledger;
- Phase 2 : sales and purchase ledgers;
- Phase 3 : sales invoicing and stock control;
- Phase 4 : sales order processing;
- Phase 5 : purchase order processing;
- Phase 6 : payroll and fixed assets.

The concept is to implement and consolidate (in practical rather than accounting terms) each element of the system before taking on another. Starting in the 'middle' (ie with the nominal ledger), the above scenario shows the implementation 'spreading out' to take in, first the closely related personal ledger systems and then moving on to the sales related elements, followed by the purchase related module with, finally, two more or less independent modules being taken aboard.

The above plan is by no means sacrosanct and it can obviously be adjusted for different circumstances. For example, many people prefer to start with the sales and stock activities, perhaps feeling that they are getting a more immediate benefit from their new system. The concept, however, is that the system is implemented a step or two at a time, with each new step being taken with the confidence that the system implemented thus far is fully operational and understood. To use a building analogy, the aim is to build each storey of the house on a firm foundation.

Parallel running

One of the favoured methods for the introduction of an accounting system, parallel running nevertheless places a considerable burden on those who have to implement and control operations. Taken at its extreme, parallel running implies that two complete systems are run concurrently, ie that all input made to the existing system must be replicated in the proposed system. The timetable is, therefore, as follows:

- set up all master file details on new system;
- set up opening transaction position on new system;
- prove conversion;
- make transaction input to old system;
- make same transaction input to new system;
- print reports from old system;
- print same or equivalent reports from new system;
- compare results from reports.

Unless volumes are fairly small, parallel running can be a difficult operation to control, particularly if staff are already well stretched in coping with the current system. The problems of ensuring that the same transactions are entered to both systems (and, remember, this will include the same maintenance of master file details) will be compounded by the differences which are almost bound to exist between the two systems. Indeed, some of these differences may make the parallel running exercise almost pointless. For example, the rounding on VAT calculations in two sales invoicing systems may differ such that the entry of invoices on the sales ledger of those systems will no longer be directly comparable. Similarly, the calculation of discounts on an automated payments run in the purchase ledger can also lead to discrepancies.

The additional workload of a parallel run may not be limited merely to the replication of the input and a reconciliation of control totals. This may well be the case if the exercise goes smoothly, but if a problem is encountered in the new (or perhaps even worse, in the old) system further time may need to be invested to get back on course. Any discrepancies between the systems will need to be investigated (yet more time) and possibly correcting input may be required (even more time).

Despite all this, if the resources are available, parallel running can be the most judicious way of introducing a new system. It has the obvious advantage of enabling a complete reconciliation between the old and new methods and confidence will be engendered in both management and staff that not only can the new system handle all the work of the old, but also, hopefully, there are other advantages to be gained in terms of speed, ease of input and quality of information.

The length of the parallel run need not be too long, indeed, if the first month's work can be reconciled between the two systems this may be considered to be a sufficient proving of the new system and the installation can then 'go live' in the following month. If, however, problems arise in the first month it may be felt that a second month of 'clean' running would be in order before effecting the changeover. Whatever strategy is adopted, there should be some idea in mind of the length of time for which parallel running is to be allowed. Some users are so attached to their old systems, or possibly fearful of the new, that parallel running continues for months on end and there can be little purpose in this. A better way of looking at things would be to legislate for, say, a period of three months of parallel running, this being sufficient time to have gained a 'clean' month; if all goes well before this it may be decided to abandon the old system before the end of the projected three-month period.

If major problems are experienced in the new system or, even after three months, an acceptable level of operation has not been obtained then it may be better to call the parallel run to a halt and to start again at a later date when the problems have been resolved (or the new system changed!). This does, of course, imply another conversion process, but this may still be preferable to prolonging the agony of a troubled parallel run and it will permit you to withdraw from the front line and give you time to rethink your strategy 'behind the lines'.

When the decision is taken to go live on the new system care should be taken to define at which point the old system is deemed to have ceased operation and the new system started, ie which are to be considered the true accounting records for the period of the parallel run. In theory, the new system is operational only at the end of the exercise but, if all has gone well, it may be decided to use the new system's records in entirety, ie from the start of the parallel run. Whatever is decided, a proper reconciliation should be drawn between the old and new systems at that point so that the continuity of the accounting records is demonstrably ensured.

Pilot running

Pilot running seeks to avoid the heavy resource implications of parallel running while still ensuring that confidence can be gained in the new system. Pilot running lends itself principally to organizations in which there are a number of separately identifiable units for which separate accounting records are maintained such as, for example, one company in a multi-company organization. This unit will be converted to the new system while the rest (and majority) of the organization continues to operate under the old regime.

The timetable is as follows:

- set up master file details for pilot;
- enter opening transaction position for pilot;

- prove conversion for pilot;
- run old system for non-pilot;
- run new system for pilot;
- set up master file details for non-pilot;
- enter opening position for non-pilot;
- prove conversion for non-pilot.

Pilot running can ease the strain of implementing a new system by confining all the problems (if, indeed there are any) to a small and well-defined area, while the rest of the organization's accounting is carried out in the normal way on the old system. When the pilot run has proved itself, the rest of the accounting entities can follow down what is now a hopefully well-established path. Because there are far fewer implications in terms of commitment of resources, pilot running can be mooted for a much longer period than parallel running and neither is the penalty for abandoning the process so severe.

With all this going for it, it is surprising that pilot running is not adopted more often in the implementation of an accounts system, although it does require the existence of a relatively small and autonomous accounting entity within an organization, something which is not always available. The other principal drawbacks are that pilot running does not deal with the volumes which will need to be processed through the live system (and these volumes may have implications for disk capacity or speed of processing) and there may still be some circumstances which will not have been processed through the pilot system as it is only a microcosm of the 'real world' of your data. Nevertheless, if viable, pilot running is a good means of establishing confidence in the new system and, to some extent, of smoothing the conversion process.

Direct changeover

Despite the textbook advocacies for parallel or pilot running, many users, particularly those with a relatively small accounts workload, favour the direct changeover method. The purists may well turn their noses up at this but, if the new system is a well-proven and well-understood (by the user) package and the user has had some experience of computerized accounting systems then this method is quite likely to work. Indeed, there are some advantages to a timetable which will read something like:

- set up master file data for new system;
- enter opening position;
- prove conversion;
- GO!

The danger, of course, is that the user is exposed if things do not work out well or if something unexpected happens. The amount of risk is to a large extent dependent upon the volume of processing; some organizations could recover quite easily if it were necessary to re-enter and reprocess a month's worth of transactions whereas, for others, this would be a major exercise, tantamount to a disaster. There are advantages, however; the workload on staff is minimized and the point at which the accounting records change from one system to the other is very clear.

The direct changeover method implies confidence; confidence in yourself, your staff, the new software and the operating environment and hardware. Think carefully about whether this confidence is misplaced or based upon untested beliefs. Then think about what would happen if, at the end of the first month's processing, the new system was found to be unworkable; what would be involved in resurrecting the old system. If you are still filled with confidence at the end of all this then you will be ready to give direct changeover a go. If not, and it is far better to err on the side of safety, look towards a parallel or pilot run.

PART 4

RUNNING THE SYSTEM

9

Getting the Best from your System

BE INFORMATIVE, CONSISTENT AND ACCURATE

However similar they may be in principle, no two accounting systems are precisely the same and, other than the range and sophistication of facilities, one of the principal points of difference is likely to be the number, size and nature of the fields which are available for input. This will apply equally to master file data (such as customer names and addresses) as to transaction data (such as references and remarks). Indeed, name and address fields provide good examples of the differences which are likely to occur. In one system there may just be one name field of, say, 30 characters in length followed by 4 address fields (for 4 lines of address) also of 30 characters and a separate field for the post code. Another system may incorporate a 50 character name field and 3 lines of address specifically labelled as street, town and county and no additional post code field.

In many cases the fields available for input and their sizes are of peripheral importance (assuming a sensible minimum being provided) but, whatever is available, it is worth thinking about how you may get the best use of each field provided. This is not to say that every character of every field should be used just because it is there but rather that each field should provide you with a chance to say something more about the transaction being entered (or the customer/supplier, depending upon the type of entry). One of the biggest differences from a non-computerized ledger is that it is not always possible to go back and annotate a transaction at a later date; ie the point of entry is your one shot at entering as much information as you think may subsequently be useful.

The following paragraphs attempt to impart some useful and practical tips on input to accounting systems. Because these are of general applicability they will obviously not be right for all situations but the principles behind them are valid. In general you should remember the following.

- *Be consistent* – having established a convention, stick with it!
- *Be informative* – think of other people, less familiar with the system than you, having to look at, say, a purchase invoice transaction in isolation.

Would they know where to find the source document (ie the invoice)? Would they know the number of the batch in which it was entered? If there was a query with the customer or supplier, is there enough information to be able easily to identify the transaction to this third party?

- *Be accurate* – an obvious statement, but while great care is usually taken (and enforced by the software) with regard to value and account number fields, less attention is often given to the memorandum fields and inaccuracies of this nature can waste a lot of time at a later stage.

As well as coding conventions and the entry of individual fields, some advice is also offered on how some of the more 'tricky' accounting situations can be dealt with. This is not intended to substitute for a text on the mechanics of accounting, nor even to replace the manual of any specific product, but rather to clarify some of the situations where a computerized system may appear to differ from its manual counterpart. Again, this advice should be viewed in the context that different options may be available in certain systems and that these cannot therefore be instructions which are cast in stone. Nevertheless, this advice will hopefully prove useful for those who wish to understand the principles of how these situations can be dealt with and this should help to make the practice that much easier.

TIPS ON INPUT

Customer and supplier files

Use of sundry account records

Unless you particularly wish to do so, it is not normally necessary to set up an individual account record for absolutely every customer or supplier with whom you deal. While there is nothing actually wrong with this practice (and, particularly for customers, you may in any case require details to be held as part of a large sales database), it can lead to unnecessarily large master files with the majority of records being redundant in terms of being required again in the future. In reality, therefore, many users of purchase and sales ledgers operate a sundry or miscellaneous accounts record(s) into which transactions of the following types may be posted:

- one-off (or at least low volume) customers or suppliers with whom an extended period of credit is not anticipated;
- customers or suppliers with whom cash (as opposed to credit) sales or purchases are conducted;
- customers or suppliers with whom low value (as well as relatively low volume) transactions are conducted ('low value' will of course be subjective, but say anything less than £100 as a guideline).

The use which is made of such accounts (if any) is discretionary, but remember that all account records (which tend in any case to be large because of fields such as name and address) are likely to attract the same system overhead in terms of storage space and also the increase in access and file passing times. Hence, within reason, it will pay to keep the master files trimmed down as far as is possible.

Having said this, there is little point in creating a monster of a sundry accounts account which is full of unmatched transactions and becomes a nightmare to reconcile or control. If there is a large number of transactions for many different customers/suppliers then it will be worth creating more than one such sundry account, eg:

- sundry accounts A to F;
- sundry accounts G to M;
- sundry accounts N to S;
- sundry accounts T to Z;

the account to which a particular transaction is posted being determined alphabetically from the customer's or supplier's name. This can be carried even further by having a sundry accounts record for each letter of the alphabet.

If, even with an alphabetic subdivision, any account of this nature becomes difficult to control then it is counterproductive and it will be better to admit defeat, set up as many new specific accounts as is necessary and journal the relevant transactions out of the sundry account and into the new one. It is never worth sacrificing expediency for control.

Account number

Probably more than anywhere else, some thought devoted to the definition of customer and supplier account coding conventions can pay back in terms of ease of use and clarity for years to come. Remember that you will come to know many of your suppliers and customers by their account numbers and that they will be keyed in innumerable times over the lifetime of a system. Additionally, much of the system's reporting is likely to be in account number order and hence it is useful to dictate some degree of logic into this. Some pointers in this vital area follow.

1. If you have an existing numbering convention which is compatible with the new system then, unless you have a particularly good reason to change, it is well worth retaining it. It will be one new thing fewer for you and your staff to get used to and it may well help to ease the continuity between the two systems, particularly during pilot or parallel running.
2. If you are inventing a new numbering system, try to use a method which has some alphabetic basis, eg:

   A010 – Aardvark and Co
   A020 – Abacus and Co
   A030 – Albert and Co
   A999 – Sundry accounts for letter A
   B010 – Badger and Co

   Many sales and purchase ledger reports are produced in account number order and it helps considerably to tie this in with the customer or supplier name in this way. An increment of ten is left between each account within each letter so that new accounts can be consistently accommodated at a later stage; for example Adder and Co may subsequently be added as account number A025. Depending upon the number of characters available and the volume of accounts, this type of coding system can be refined, eg:

AAR001 – Aardvark and Co
ABA001 – Abacus and Co
ALB001 – Albert and Co
AZZ999 – Sundry accounts for letter A
BAD001 – Badger and Co

or as:

A0100 – Aardvark and Co
A0200 – Abacus and Co
A0300 – Albert and Co
A9999 – Sundry accounts for letter A
B0100 – Badger and Co

The point of the exercise is to make for ease of visual recognition and logical reporting sequences and remember that, having embarked upon a particular course, it will not be at all easy to change at some stage in the future.

3. In relation to the alphabetic significance of account coding, think carefully what you will want to do with account names such as 'W G Aardvark and Co'. Will you want this to appear under 'W' or 'A'? Whatever you decide, try to ensure that the rule is applied consistently throughout.
4. Keep the length and formats of the account numbers you use consistent and remember that you do not necessarily have to use all the characters provided up to the maximum length of the field. If you have only one hundred suppliers, a six character account code is probably something of an overkill even though the only identifiable saving may be in terms of the number of keys that will need to be pressed over the lifetime of the system. Ensure that all account numbers are of the same length and format; the following are not good examples of supplier or customer account numbering:

AARD – Aardvark and Co
ABA – Abacus and Co
ALB – Albert and Co
BADG1 – Badger and Co
BADG2 – Badge Products and Co

5. In general it is not a good idea to reuse an account number when the original account record has been closed. Some systems will in any case not permit this, but your chosen coding system should not leave you so short of possible numbers that there is not another that you can use. Even if the system does permit it (as it may well do if the file has been purged, say at

end of year), it is still not a good idea and is a potential avenue for confusion when looking at reports from different accounting periods.

6. If there are sundry accounts on the ledger and they are not coded by individual letter, you may think it sensible not only to group them together but also to position them at the end of the file in terms of account code order reporting sequences. Hence rather than code 'sundry accounts' as SUN001, SUN002, etc for example, it may be more useful to code them as ZZZ001, ZZZ002, etc. This is not a major point but, again, it all helps to make the ledger more manageable as time goes on.
7. Note that if you start account codes with numbers these will generally appear in reports before any which start with letters, ie:

7BEL01 – 7 Bells Pub AARD01 – Aardvark and Co ABAC01 – Abacus and Co ALBE01 – Albert and Co BADG01 – Badger and Co

While on the subject of numbers, remember that the letters 'I' and 'O' can often cause confusion with the numbers '1' and '0'. This can be mitigated by any particular character position always being alphabetic or numeric in nature.

8. If you can possibly avoid it, try not to use the same account numbers on both sales and purchase ledgers. Similarly, if there are a number of companies in operation, avoid the duplication of account numbers between them. This practice reduces the risk of entry of a transaction into the wrong ledger and makes clear, merely by noting the account number, as to which part of the accounting set-up the account relates.

Name, address and post code

Name and address fields are occasionally a source of problems in an accounts system which, given that they are held principally for memorandum purposes, is quite surprising. The format of the name, address and post code fields will be dictated to a large extent by the software product being used but, whatever it is, there are advantages to being consistent with your input and that means deciding from the outset, unless you would like a substantial rekeying exercise at a later stage. Bear in mind these considerations.

- From a cosmetic viewpoint, be consistent with use of upper and lower case for all names and addresses. If you think that you or your staff cannot do this then stick to upper case for everything.
- Be wary of punctuation. Users who are new to computer systems frequently key names and addresses as though they were on a typewriter, even down to the comma at the end of each line. While the effect is subjective, punctuation can look messy on computer produced documents. Another deterrent is that, in certain circumstances, punctuation can even cause incorrect processing such as, for example, where an address field containing a comma is output to a file in another system (eg a word processing package) which uses commas to delineate between fields.

- ☐ In an integrated accounts system, the address is likely to be used for customer statements, purchase ledger remittance advice notes, sales invoices and sales and purchase order documentation. Think about how you would like these addresses to appear and then, if applicable, consider outside uses such as labels and interface to word processing for debtors letters or, more positively, mailshots. This may dictate how much you enter on each line.
- ☐ Think of any possibilities for the use of the address field for customer or supplier analysis. The prime field to consider here is obviously the post code field, but if, for example, you were consistent in your input such that the town was always entered in line three of the address (even if that means leaving line two blank), then you may be able to open up other possibilities.

Other customer/supplier master file fields

In general, most other master file fields will be of a memorandum nature (such as contact names and telephone numbers), an analysis nature (such as representative codes) or will relate to trading conditions (such as credit limits or discount percentages) to be used by related systems.

If you do not think that you will ever use these fields, do not feel constrained to complete them just because they appear on the screen, particularly as you can use amendment facilities to enter or reset them at a later stage if you change your mind. You should, however, always be on the lookout for extra information which can be obtained from the accounts system and master file contact details, for example, can provide useful and time-saving listings for general distribution. In this respect, some systems recognize the value of this by providing not only contact details for the accounts departments, but also for sales and purchasing contacts. It may take time to establish and set up but, once done, you will stand to gain thereafter.

Personal ledger transaction files

General

As with master file input, the fields available for transaction entry will vary between systems as will the size and nature of the data allowed within them. The following fields will, however, be available in most systems. Again, what you decide to enter in these fields, if anything, will largely be discretionary and the following are merely suggestions as to their use. Do remember, however, the point made earlier that, unlike a manual ledger card, when leaving any field blank you will not be able to come back and add something to the entry at a later date.

Anything entered which helps to identify the transaction, not only to you but also to the customer or supplier, may save considerable time at a later stage and can even, in extreme cases, help to prevent overpayments or underpayments from occurring, for example by noting that you have been invoiced twice for the same service. Remember once again to be consistent. Having determined the use to which a particular field will be put, ensure that you keep to it and, if appropriate, include it in the supplementary instructions which you prepare for your staff.

'Our reference' field

For sales ledger invoice input this will be the sales invoice number. For purchase ledger invoices the internal serial (or logging) number applied on receipt of the invoice may be used, otherwise the supplier's invoice number will suffice.

For sales cash input, the cash book folio (ie page number) is as good as anything. Attempts to standardize on entry of the invoice number to which the receipt relates meet a sticky end when a customer pays 15 invoices by the same cheque! For purchase ledger cash input, use the cheque number.

'Your (ie customer/supplier's) reference'

This type of field can be useful in supplementary identification. For sales invoices, the customer's order reference is a sensible use, the only difficulty being that some organizations have order numbers which are far larger than anything which may be provided for this type of field. If an internal sequence numbering system is used for purchase invoices then the supplier's invoice number is an obvious possibility for this field.

Transaction date

This should be fairly straightforward as most systems will provide a data vet for a valid date format. Probably the main consideration is that, for sales and purchase invoices, the date entered is likely to be used as the basis of its position in calculations for ageing analysis and, in the case of a purchase ledger invoice, for payment. Normally this would not be a problem but if, for example, a purchase invoice is received in May but is dated January this would be likely to be triggered immediately in any automatic payments run. This may not matter in specific circumstances, but it is something you should be aware of. In such a situation, a solution can be reached by entering a current date for the transaction but noting the real date of the invoice in the remarks field.

Remarks

Most ledger systems allow for some text to be entered for a transaction and this is potentially one of the most important fields in a system. While it is possible manually to annotate the printout produced from a computerized system this will eventually be superseded by a further printout (eg for the following period) and the annotation must be made again or lost. The contrast between this scenario and that in a non-computerized system has already been highlighted.

The remarks or comments field is hence effectively *the* chance to annotate the ledger in a computerized system and, once bypassed, the opportunity may be lost forever! Think carefully before leaving such a field blank – is there really nothing further to say about a transaction which will not help identify or clarify it at a later date, if not to you then somebody else? Remarks can range from a brief description of the goods or services, customer or supplier reference numbers (where these are too large to be held in the 'your reference' fields) or, in the case of sundry accounts, the name of the customer or supplier. For purchase invoices, the goods received note (GRN) number and/or purchase order number may be applicable; for sales invoices, the customer order number. Again, consistency in the use of remarks is preferable, but any use is better than none.

Nominal master file

Nominal account coding (and cost centres)

Many companies have corporately defined nominal coding structures and the ability of a particular system to accommodate such a specific structure will have been a principal selection criterion. If you are in any doubt as to how you should proceed it is worth consulting with your auditors as it is they who will also have a vested interest in the way in which the nominal ledger is constructed.

Here are some general points to note.

- □ Nominal codes are normally numerically based as there is little virtue in having a trial balance, for example, which is produced on an alphabetic basis. Even in the event that alphabetic characters are permitted, it is generally suggested that a numeric-only convention is adopted unless, for example, there is an alphabetic indicator to denote the type of account.
- □ Many systems will permit hierarchical structuring of the nominal code and it is worth investigating how you may benefit from this; do not, however, be tempted to define a nominal coding with a structure more complicated than your needs as this will become a burden which you will have to bear for a long time for no real advantage.
- □ Always define nominal codes with intervals between code numbers so that there is ample scope for adding new codes without upsetting the logical structure of the accounts.
- □ Always group like accounts together; not only does this have advantages in reviewing output, it is also likely to make the definition of user-definable reports, such as profit and loss and balance sheets, much easier as they can then be referenced by range of accounts rather than the individual nomination of each constituent account.
- □ A typical overall coding structure would be something like:

CODE	DESCRIPTION	TYPE OF ACCOUNT
100/	Sales	P & L
200/	Purchases	P & L
300/	Marketing	P & L
400/	Establishment	P & L
500/	Finance	P & L
600/	Fixed assets	Bal sheet
700/	Current assets	Bal sheet
800/	Current liabilities	Bal sheet
900/	Finance and equity	Bal sheet

Within each of the above headings there may be a series of sub-codes for more detailed analysis, such as:

100/	Sales
100/001	Sales of product A
100/002	Sales of product B
or:	
800/	Current liabilities
800/100	Trade creditors
800/200	Sundry creditors and accruals
800/300	VAT control
800/400	PAYE control

and so on.

Such a system lends itself to easy definition for profit and loss and balance sheet report definition and makes the nature of each account instantly identifiable from the first few characters.

The restriction of numeric characters should not necessarily be applied to cost centres, departments or whatever type of alternative analysis codes are provided for nominal ledger transactions. In general these should be made as meaningful as possible and there is a distinct advantage in using non-numeric codes so that they can be easily distinguished, such as:

WIN	Winchester depot;
COL	Colchester depot;
ROC	Rochester depot;
CHQ	Central headquarters cost centre.

Nominal transaction files

Transaction reference

In nominal ledger input the reference field will normally be self-explanatory, being a journal number, a cash book folio (ie page) number or something similar.

Transaction date

Again, this is a field which is fairly obvious, but it is important to note whether the date of an entry will affect the period attaching to the transaction in the system or whether this function is performed by a separate period number field.

Remarks

Just as the remarks field in the personal ledgers were flagged as significant, so the same applies for the equivalent field in the nominal ledger. There must be *something* which can be said about each nominal transaction; if not, once it is posted to the ledger it will be too late if you think of it later!

10

Entry of specific situations

In this chapter advice is offered on how some of the more 'tricky' accounting situations can be dealt with. This is not intended to be a substitute for a text on the mechanics of accounting, nor even to replace the manual of any specific product, but rather to clarify some of the situations when a computerized system may appear to differ from its manual counterpart. Again, this advice should be viewed in the context that different options may be available in certain systems and that these cannot therefore be instructions which are cast in stone. Nevertheless, this advice will hopefully prove useful for those who wish to understand the principles of how these situations can be dealt with and this should help to make the practice that much easier.

TRANSACTION TYPES

Most accounting systems attempt to help the user by providing a number of ready-made transaction types for entry to the system, thus preventing, if at all possible, the need to sort out the debits from the credits. Indeed, it would be a poor system if, say, the sales ledger did not include a specific purpose sales invoice input stream, relieving the user of the need to remember whether invoices should debit or credit individual customer accounts. A summary of the principal transaction types which are commonly found was given in Chapter 2, but some packages go far beyond the basics and try to allow for many eventualities, and there are even those which permit users to define their own transaction types.

The situations which follow may not, therefore, always pose a problem as there may be a welcoming option on the menu designed to address just the specific circumstance. Just in case there is not such an option in your system, and you are unsure of the accounting principles involved, the following may provide some guidance as to how the transaction may be addressed. Remember that, as with so much advice of a general nature, there is likely to be more than just the one way of effecting a solution.

Many of the following examples involve the use of a journal adjustment type of transaction stream within the sales and purchase ledgers. This is meant to refer to an input mechanism which is distinct from invoices or credit notes (or cash) and in which it is possible to define the entry as being a credit or a debit to the nominated customer or supplier account. If your system does not incorporate such a transaction type then, less than optimally, you may have to use the invoice or credit note input stream in its stead.

Opening balances on sales and purchase ledgers

One of the most frequently encountered problems facing the first-time (or even subsequent) user of accounting systems is the setting up of an opening position in the sales and purchase ledgers. Some systems provide a special stream of transaction entry to cater for this but, even where this is so, some understanding of the principles behind the operation are required.

To set a practical tone, imagine that our new system is to start on 1 May 19xx and that all outstanding purchase and sales invoices as at 30 April 19xx are to be keyed into the new system. Say that, on the purchase ledger, our good friends Aardvark and Co have an invoice dated 1 February 19xx. The details of this invoice were as follows:

Account	: AAR001 (Aardvark and Co)
Invoice date	: 1 February 19xx
Gross value	: £235
VAT value	: £35
Nominal analysis	
Purchase of parts	: £180
Delivery charges	: £20

First, consider the effect of entering this as a normal purchase invoice in the new system, ie as at 1 May 19xx. The effect on the purchase ledger would be:

	Dr	**Cr**
Aardvark & Co		235
PL control account	235	

So far, so good; this is exactly what we want to achieve on the purchase ledger.But what about the nominal? Here the entries would be:

	Dr	**Cr**
Purchase of parts	180	
Delivery	20	
VAT control	35	
Creditors control		235

We would not want this to happen. To start with, the expenditure on purchase of parts and delivery has already been accounted for in the old system, as has the VAT input. We do not want these items to be counted twice. Additionally, a set of opening balances (ie as at 1 May 19xx) will be entered to the nominal ledger at some stage and these will include a figure for creditors control which will incorporate this £235 in respect of Aardvark and Co; hence there is a danger also of the creditor being double counted.

In effect, we are just interested in setting up the liability on the purchase ledger and doing nothing else. So, the transaction will become:

ACCOUNT	: AAR001 (Aardvark and Co)
Invoice date	: 1 February 19xx
Gross value	: £235
VAT value	: £0
Nominal analysis	
Creditors control	: £235

Thus, the transaction should be entered such that its effect on the nominal ledger will be self-cancelling, the real creditors control balance being set up by the opening balances journal entered to the nominal ledger. (It will, of course, still be vital that this balance is reconciled with the control account balance in the purchase ledger itself.) The accounting entries in the purchase ledger remain as:

	Dr	**Cr**
Aardvark & Co		235
PL control account	235	

But, in the nominal, the entries are simply:

	Dr	**Cr**
Creditors control	235	
Creditors control		235

The same principle applies to opening transactions on the sales ledger and the same comments about the reconciliation between the sales ledger control account and the debtors control account in the nominal ledger apply.

Needless to say, transactions occurring on or after 1 May 19xx should be keyed in normally so that normal nominal ledger accounting takes place on the new system thereafter.

Opening nominal ledger balances

The entry of an opening position to the nominal ledger should effectively be equivalent to a trial balance type of journal as at the closing date of the old system. This can be entered as an ordinary journal to the nominal ledger. In practice, the final set of balances may not be available until some time after the new system has gone live, but this should not matter as the journal can be set up whenever it becomes ready.

The points already made about the need to reconcile the debtors and creditors control accounts with, respectively, the sales and purchase ledgers should not be forgotten and this reconciliation should be made as at the effective date of implementation of the new system, although any transactions processed subsequently should still leave the reconciliation intact. Similarly, the balance on the bank account(s) should be reconcilable with the cash book(s).

If the system in use has a fairly low limit to the maximum number of lines permitted in a single journal entry, this may cause a problem if the number of accounts to be included in the opening balance journal is large. This can be easily circumvented by splitting the journal into a number of constituent parts, each one of which is balanced by an entry to a suspense (or, more accurately, a journal control) account. Indeed, this may not be a bad idea for the entry of any large journal as it can help to make the input more manageable, particularly in systems which do not easily cope with the display of large journals (eg those larger than a single screen). At the end of the exercise, of course, the balance on the suspense account should be zero, being formed merely of the balancing entries for each constituent part of a journal which is balanced overall.

Accruals and prepayments

Accruals are items which occasionally puzzle non-accountants and the following general advice can be given: 'if you do not understand what accruals are, then do not use any facilities relating to them'. In effect an accrual is an adjustment to the accounts for a specific period in respect of known items for which no accounting entry has yet been made.

A simple example can be built around the payment of rent. If rent is £120,000 per annum, paid quarterly in arrears, then the cash payments of £30,000 would be shown in the monthly accounts only for those months it which it was actually paid, ie an accounting entry would normally be made only when the cash transactions were effected. In the preparation of accounts for other months, however, it would be necessary to take the proportion of the rent into consideration to satisfy the fundamental accounting principle of revenue matching expenditure for a given time span and hence the need for an accrual to reflect this acknowledged, but as yet unpaid, debt. An accrual is, therefore, raised to record this liability and this transaction is reversed in the following period to revert the accounts back to their original state.

The more sophisticated systems provide facilities which cater for the automatic reversal of accruals (and prepayments) in the period following that in which they were entered. In such systems, the accrual will be identified as a specific transaction type and the entry made in a similar fashion to nominal journals. The accrual will appear as such on the end of period nominal reports and be included in balances but, on ending the period, the transaction will be reversed so that its effect is nullified for the start of the next period. Ideally, this will be clearly shown as a discrete transaction on the ledger so that a complete trail of processing can be maintained. If, for example, an accrual was entered in period N as:

	Dr	Cr
Rent	10,000	
Sundry creditors		10,000

then the start of period N+1 would see a reversal of this transaction, ie

	Dr	Cr
Rent		10,000
Sundry creditors	10,000	

At the end of period N+1 a further accrual may be entered, this time for £20,000 (£10,000 of which would relate specifically to period N+1), and this would be reversed at the start of period N+2. Finally, in period N+2, the cash payment of £30,000 would be made. The net effect of all this on the rent account would be as follows:

		Dr	Cr
Period N	: Accrual	10,000	
Period N+1	: Reversal		10,000
Period N+1	: Accrual	20,000	
Period N+2	: Reversal		20,000
Period N+2	: Cash Payment	30,000	

The balance on the rent account would then be £30,000 Dr and the amount taken into each period's accounting £10,000 Dr, precisely what is required. Prepayments are the accounting opposite of accruals and would apply, for example, if the rent were paid quarterly in advance rather than in arrears; the same principles apply in all other respects.

Where automatic accrual processing facilities do not exist there is nothing to prevent the same exercise being mirrored by the entry of journals; first for the entry of the accrual in the first period and then for the reversal in the second period. Naturally, the reference and remarks fields should be properly utilized to make the nature of these journals clear. This does, of course, imply twice as much work, compared with the automatic reversal of accruals and it also carries the risk of the reversal being effected incorrectly but it does mean that, if a particular system is adequate in other respects, the lack of accrual facilities can at least be worked around.

Contra entries between sales and purchase ledgers

Where a company is both a customer and supplier, ie is present on both sales and purchase ledgers, it is occasionally necessary to set off part or all of the balance on one ledger against that of the other. This is a practice which is more prevalent in some industries than others and some systems provide specific facilities for it which may effectively generate a journal directly between the debtors and creditors control accounts in the nominal ledger to reflect the transfer of a balance from one ledger to the other.

Where no automatic facility is provided, the operation can be effectively carried out and controlled by the means of separate input into the purchase and sales ledgers and the use of a 'contra control' type of account on the nominal ledger. Take, as an example, the contra of £235 from a sales ledger account to a purchase ledger account. In the sales ledger the following input can be made, preferably by means of a journal or adjustment type of transaction:

SALES LEDGER

Account	: AAR001 (Aardvark and Co)
Adjustment date	: 1 February 19xx
Gross value	: £235
Debit/credit	: Credit (to sales ledger)
Remarks	: CONTRA TO AAR001 ON PL
Nominal analysis	
Contra control	: £235 (debit)

Similarly, the adjustment entered to the purchase ledger would be:

PURCHASE LEDGER

Account	: AAR001 (Aardvark and Co)
Adjustment date	: 1 February 19xx
Gross value	: £235
Debit/credit	: Debit (to purchase ledger)
Remarks	: CONTRA FROM AAR001 ON SL
Nominal analysis	
Contra control	: £235 (credit)

Note that the contra has no effect on VAT and the transaction should be performed purely in gross terms, in effect one debt is being set off against another.

The contra control account in the nominal ledger should always clear to zero and any balance on this account would imply that only one side of a contra transaction had been effected or that one of the entries had been made incorrectly and would hence require investigation. In the above example this account would show:

	Dr	Cr
From sales ledger	235	
From purchase ledger		235

In systems where there is no adjustment type of transaction then the above entries could be effected by using a credit note entry to both ledgers, although the transactions would need to be referenced in such a way as to make it clear that these were not normal credit note items.

Exchange differences

Systems with multi-currency options would normally find that exchange differences are calculated and accounted for automatically as and when they are encountered following the discrepancy found between the sterling equivalent of the cash entered to the sales or purchase ledger and that of the invoices which are being paid.

Exchange differences are also a fact of life on systems which are being run in a single currency (such as sterling), particularly as markets and sources widen internationally. There are two principal methods for dealing with such situations:

(A) enter all transactions, including the exchange difference, through the personal ledger; or
(B) force a balance with the invoice(s) in the personal ledger and post the exchange difference direct to the nominal ledger.

Take as a simple example a purchase invoice for 10,000 Deutschmarks. This amount would need to be converted to sterling at the time of entry of the invoice to the system at whatever exchange rate is considered appropriate at that point. At some later stage, the invoice will need to be paid, the supplier requiring payment in the native currency. By that time the exchange rate will have moved and, assuming that no other policy has been adopted in respect of dealing with exchange differences, the sterling equivalent of the 10,000DM paid will differ from the amount actually held on the purchase ledger.

If, say, the invoice for 10,000DM converted to £4,100 and the payment to £4,000, then method (A) above would imply cash book entries as follows:

	TOTAL PAYMENT	PURCHASE LEDGER
xx Feb 19xx Aardvark and Co	4,000	4,000

and the following entries appearing in the purchase ledger:

Account AAR001 : Aardvark and Co

	Dr	Cr
1. Invoice		4,100
2. Payment	4,000	
3. Adjustment	100	

The value entered is for the sterling equivalent at the time of the payment and a separate adjustment entry must be made for the exchange difference (being analysed to an exchange difference account in the nominal ledger). This method has the advantage that a complete record of the transaction can be seen on the supplier record, but there is a disadvantage in the need for an extra input being required for each payment affected (ie in respect of the adjustment) and this additional transaction may also complicate the allocation process when matching off payments against invoices.

Method (B) implies the following cash book entries:

	TOTAL PAYMENT	PURCHASE LEDGER	EXCHANGE DIFFERENCE
xx Feb 19xx Aardvark and Co	4,000	4,100	(100)

and the following entries appearing in the purchase ledger:

Account AAR001 : Aardvark and Co

	Dr	Cr
1. Invoice		4,100
2. Payment	4,100	

This makes for a cleaner situation in the purchase ledger where, after all, the main intention is to establish the extent of debt to the supplier. The exchange difference is posted directly to the nominal ledger (debit bank, credit exchange differences in the above example as the exchange difference is favourable, but vice versa if it were adverse) or, if desired, the sum of the exchange differences for the period can be posted as one transaction in the period end cash book journal. The disadvantage of this approach is that the bank account in the nominal ledger contains entries which need to be combined to effect agreement with the specific cheque amounts but, provided that an overall reconciliation is achieved, this should not present too great a problem.

Discounts received/allowed

Most systems will cater for prompt settlement discounts being taken on entry of cash into the sales and purchase ledgers. The discount is analyzed to the nominated account on the nominal ledger (discounts received for purchase ledger, discounts allowed for sales ledger) and the entry is shown on the personal ledger. For example, a purchase ledger account might show:

	Dr	Cr
1. Invoice		235
2. Payment (this being the actual cheque amount)	230	
3. Discount taken	5	

If no automatic facility is available the latter transaction will need to be entered separately as an adjustment and the three transactions can then be successfully allocated. The discount transaction would be a debit to the supplier account (and credit discounts received) for the purchase ledger and a credit to the customer account (and debit discounts allowed) for the sales ledger. It is, of course, important always to enter the cash as the actual value of the cheque received or paid (ie as £230 in the above example) and not to be tempted to gross it up to include the discount value.

Discounts disallowed

As the term implies, discounts disallowed occur when you have taken advantage of a prompt settlement discount, but the supplier has deemed that payment was not received in time to qualify for the reduced payment. In this event your purchase ledger account for that supplier may contain:

	Dr	Cr
1. Invoice		235
2. Payment	230	
3. Discount taken	5	

The discounts received account in the nominal ledger would then reflect this £5 as a credit entry.

The subsequent disallowal of the discount would require that it be reinstated on the supplier account and this would need to be effected by an adjustment facility with the nominal analysis being made to the discounts received account, ie:

Value : £5
Nominal analysis
Discounts received £5 (debit)

The purchase ledger would now show:

	Dr	Cr
1. Invoice		235
2. Payment	230	
3. Discount taken	5	
4. Discount disallowed		5

ie a liability of £5 would have been reinstated and the discounts received account on the nominal ledger would clear to zero, assuming no other transactions were involved.

Bad debts

The writing off of bad debts from the sales ledger (and, by a similar token, the write-off of unsettled amounts from the purchase ledger) is again normally effected through an adjustment facility to credit the relevant customer account with the nominal analysis being made to the bad debts account (if it is, in fact, a bad debt), to a relevant sales or purchase account or, in respect of significant amounts which are before the current financial year, to a separately identifiable account for the purpose.

Cash refunds

Cash refunds (ie payments made through the sales ledger or receipts to the purchase ledger) can cause confusion in the inexperienced and this sometimes results in strange forms of entry being made. Some systems will provide a separate input stream for these relatively rare events. If not, one option is to enter them through the normal cash input facility, but with a negative sign on the amount; this assumes, of course, that the system will permit such an entry.

The other alternative is again to use an adjustment facility, for example for a sales ledger cash refund:

Account AAR001	: Aardvark & Co
Value	: £235
Debit/credit	: Debit
Nominal analysis	
Bank account	: £235 (credit)

The sales ledger account would thus look like this:

	Dr	Cr
1. Invoice	235	
2. Payment received		235
3. Cash refund	235	

In this example it is likely that a credit note would be issued to the customer to clear the account (assuming, for example, that the goods for which the payment was originally received had been returned) but, in the event of the customer having mistakenly paid an invoice twice (and these things do happen occasionally), the entry of the cash refund would be sufficient to return the balance to zero.

11

Practical Operation of the System

THE MINUTIAE OF ACCOUNTING

Many people think that accounting is not the most thrilling of disciplines and this school of thought was encapsulated some years ago by the famous advertisement for a well-known brand of vodka which ran: 'I used to be an accountant, until I discovered. . .' The advances in computing technology during the 1980s, much of it with financial applications and staff at the forefront, has done much to give accounting a much brighter and up-to-date image. The graphical user interfaces (GUIs) and diagrammatic output added during the 1990s has served to enhance this still further. Nevertheless, even with the new technology, there is still routine work to be carried out in order to form the grist to the accounting mill, so much of the detail of this chapter is given over to the minutiae of accounting, such as the filing of invoices, the printing of reports (some of which may take an appreciable amount of time, a fact not always recognized by those who are new to accounting) and the scheduling of input of transactions. Never mind; it is the attention given to details such as these which make the difference between well and badly run accounts departments and enable the accountant to step boldly into the realms of information management in a wider context, secure in the knowledge of the reliability of his base information.

Most experienced accountants can tell within minutes of walking into an accounts office whether it is being run under, or out of, control. Tell-tale signs of disorganization and untidiness, such as mounds of loose invoices in messy piles, reports bursting out of binders or scattered randomly on the floor, frequent and hot debates on the telephone with suppliers and/or customers and ledgers which are weeks (or even months) behind the current date all give clues that everything may not be well. It should be recognized that a computerized system may even add to the burden by the volume of paper produced and, although one might hesitate to admit it, the propensity occasionally for things to to go wrong, often on a grander scale than could ever be imagined with a manual system. Not all of this need necessarily be the fault of the staff, who may be overstretched and under-resourced, and the root of the problem may in fact lie at the feet of management who are unwilling or unable to put more priority into the efficient running of the function, particularly if this would entail more money or resources.

Sadly, it is all too often a vicious circle. The more an accounts system gets behind, the more time that will be spent in dealing with queries and problems such as suppliers who have not been paid or customers not being chased for payment, the effects of which can permeate through to the mainstream business such as when orders cannot be fulfilled (perhaps because suppliers are withholding delivery), or cash flow problems arise (because of customers being allowed to exceed their credit terms). There is also an increased threat of breakdowns or circumventions of control procedures which, in turn, will cause, at the very least, even more time to be wasted at some future date (such as during the statutory audit), thus leading to a further loss in time. One should not paint too bleak a picture but, particularly in companies which are subject to a rapid expansion over a short period of time, it is often the accounts systems which are the first to creak, but the last to which any attention is paid. The first step to avoid this happening, or even to start the process of catching up where it has happened, is to be clear about what should be done and when, ie to create some sense of order around the system and ensure there is the time and resources for this to be put into effect.

Whatever the pedigree of accounting system employed, the general principles of operation are similar, as are the functions which need to be performed on a routine periodic basis. Obviously the precise details will differ between organizations and the emphases placed on various activities shifted accordingly but, even so, many similarities will remain. For example, a variable factor may be that nominal ledger update may be performed daily in one company, but carried out weekly or even more infrequently elsewhere, depending perhaps upon such factors as:

- the constraints of the software;
- the division of responsibilities;
- the volume of transactions;
- how 'up-to-date' the nominal ledger is required to be at any point in time;
- not least, the personal preferences of those responsible for the ledger.

What is certain, however, is that the ledger will be updated at least once during the accounting period and that it will hence have a slot on any planned processing for the period.

The activities which follow should be taken, therefore, as guidelines rather than firm rules and should be adapted to your own working environment. For example, the requirements of a service company, perhaps with a low number of high value sales invoices, are likely to differ markedly from a supplier of computer consumables or electronic components where a high number of relatively low value transactions would be more usual. Having acknowledged the impossibility of giving universal instructions on a detailed level, there is still much to be gained by running the rule over your own accounting system procedures to see whether there is scope for improvements in efficiency or control by making adjustments at the detailed level of operation, much in the way that the general servicing of a motor car will hopefully improve its overall performance. Even systems which are well-established can benefit from such an exercise as procedures may unthinkingly have been 'handed down' across turnovers in staff and, in any event, patterns of processing may have changed radically since the system, and accompanying procedures, were introduced.

The element of 'real time' information (ie the 'up-to-date' effect noted above) required from the system will often play an important part in the definition of day-to-day procedures. For a sales ledger, it may well be important to enter and post all transactions as soon as possible after they occur so that credit control decisions can be monitored effectively and customer queries dealt with efficiently. The need may not be quite so pressing on a purchase ledger and even less so on the nominal ledger, where an 'end of period' situation is often sought rather than a continuously updated current analysis. The latter may in any case be difficult to achieve as there will normally be adjustments and accruals to be effected on the basis of the position at any given point in time.

THE ACCOUNTS TIMETABLE

The increasingly competitive commercial environment, coupled with other demands for 'instant' financial data, has generally put an ever-tightening pressure on accounts departments to produce accurate information within a short timescale, this information being an essential element of the corporate jigsaw upon which decisions are dynamically based. It is for this, if no other reason that the accounts timetable assumes such fundamental importance in many organizations as it defines, on a rolling basis, the dates at which key elements of financial information will be available. The use of such a timetable can be useful in even the smallest or most parochial of businesses as it provides a benchmark against which progress can be consistently assessed and will give the first warning if the accounting task is starting to fall behind, perhaps through a marked increase in the volume of transactions caused by a general growth in the business. In its simplest form, the accounts timetable is a template covering two accounting periods (say months) on which is marked the key points in the operation of the accounts system. Such events are likely to include:

- production of customer statements;
- production of review listing of proposed payments to suppliers;
- production of supplier cheques and remittance advice notes;
- close down date for sales ledger (not necessarily the period end date but the actual day on which the period will be closed on the system);
- cut-off date for the entry of purchase invoices;
- similarly, the close down date for the purchase ledger;
- receipt of journals, such as payroll;
- cut-off date for the calculation and entry of accruals to the nominal ledger;
- production of monthly management reports;
- close down date for the nominal ledger.

This template can then be used to define specific dates each month and the resultant timetable can be distributed to all interested parties including, it should be noted, the staff who are supposed to be working towards it. In essence, it represents a plan and there should be questions asked if the defined dates are not met; from a management viewpoint it may mean that there is a need to tackle a problem in the operation of the system or with the people or procedures around it. The problem may be connected with seasonal fluctuations in volumes, a hardware breakdown during the period, holidays or other staff absences or delays in receiving information. Whatever the explanation, it needs to be examined carefully to determine whether it is an acceptable 'one-off' or, more seriously, if it denotes a growing strain being placed upon the accounting function. If so, questions about the possibility of more staff, more input terminals (eg upgrading from single to multi-user operation), changing to a more reliable system and so on will need to be asked as it is unlikely that an increasing slippage of reporting dates will prove acceptable to those who are awaiting financial performance figures for each period.

An example of an accounts timetable is shown below; this is, of course, only an illustration and should be viewed in this light, but the principle of operation is sound and, for example, the concept of closing the period in each of the three ledgers at different times is one which will be familiar to many.

ACCOUNTS TIMETABLE : OCTOBER 19XX

Mon Oct 2 :	complete entry of September sales invoices and cash receipts;
Tue Oct 3 :	print statements, reports and close down of September sales ledger;
Thu Oct 5 :	cut-off date for receipt of September purchase invoices; complete entry of September purchase invoices and cash payments;
Fri Oct 6 :	print reports and close down of September purchase ledger;
Tue Oct 10:	cut-off date for entry of September journals/accruals; complete entry of journals, accruals and September cash book entries not covered by the sales and purchase ledgers;
Wed Oct 11:	print nominal ledger period end reports for September;
Thu Oct 12:	close down of September nominal ledger;
Fri Oct 13 :	September management accounts to Finance Director;
Wed Oct 18:	summary presentation to Board;
Mon Oct 23:	purchase ledger proposed payments listing for October;
Wed Oct 25:	purchase ledger automated payments run for October; print cheques and remittance advice notes;
Wed Nov 1 :	complete entry of October sales invoices and cash receipts;
Thu Nov 2 :	print statements, reports and close down of October sales ledger;
Mon Nov 6:	cut-off date for receipt of October purchase invoices; complete entry of October purchase invoices and cash payments and so on.

(Incidentally, it is only coincidence that the management accounts are submitted to the Finance Director on Friday the 13th, but some may appreciate the irony of this!)

No doubt there are some people who will look at the above table aghast that, even with a computerized system, September month-end accounts are not submitted until 13 October, whereas others will wonder why such a hopelessly optimistic schedule can possibly be contemplated. This only serves to illustrate the differences between organizations, accounts departments, accounting systems and, of course, accountants.

Having defined an overall framework in the form of the accounts timetable, it is possible to look at how the defined target dates may be achieved. In most systems, the various tasks lend themselves to categorization as:

- daily tasks;
- *ad hoc* tasks to be performed during the period;
- period end tasks;
- (financial) year-end tasks.

The actual category into which some tasks fall is likely to vary between organizations, but it is the concept of the operations which is important rather than the detail. The following paragraphs should be read in this context and the categories altered to suit individual circumstances and preferences.

WHAT TO DO EACH DAY

The daily tasks are those required to keep the system 'ticking over' and will primarily revolve around transaction entry, recording and filing. If this does not sound too exciting then there is little that can be done about it. If you really want to make life more exciting, you can always try *not* doing these things for a couple of months, otherwise you will need to accept that such tasks are necessary to be able to make any progress.

The amount of time required for the various tasks will be something which can be learnt from experience and, particularly in circumstances where time on the computer is limited or volumes are very high, a daily processing schedule can usefully be created. In compiling this, ensure that allowance is made for the printing and review of reports and that sufficient time is allowed for the daily backup of data, a task which will render the system universally unavailable even in a multi-user environment.

The daily activities are likely to include the following.

Sales ledger

- batching of sales invoices and credit notes, ready for input;
- input of sales invoice and credit note batches;
- batch reconciliations and maintenance of sales batch control register;
- set up customer accounts as necessary;
- filing of copy sales invoices and credit notes.

Purchase ledger

- ☐ recording of purchase invoices received, before distribution for authorization;
- ☐ batching of authorized purchase invoices and credit notes, ready for input;
- ☐ input of purchase invoice and credit note batches;
- ☐ batch reconciliations and maintenance of purchase batch control register;
- ☐ set up authorized supplier accounts as necessary;
- ☐ filing of purchase invoices and credit notes.

General

- ☐ recording and banking of cheques received;
- ☐ recording of *ad hoc* petty cash payments and receipts;
- ☐ routine daily backup.

Note that, in general, there is unlikely to be much in the way of regular daily activity on the nominal ledger other than, perhaps, *ad hoc* enquiries and reports.

WHAT TO DO DURING THE PERIOD

As well as the day-to-day activities, there are a number of other tasks which need to be performed during the course of the accounting period. These may be defined as weekly activities or may be rather more *ad hoc* and, by their nature, are likely to vary between organizations depending upon their patterns and volumes of transactions. The following list should, therefore, be taken as a very rough guide as to what might constitute 'typical' tasks.

Sales ledger

- ☐ input of sales ledger cash receipt batches (this may, of course, also be effected daily or just at the end of the period) and allocation against outstanding invoices;
- ☐ capture of transactions from sales invoicing/order processing system, if this needs to be carried out as a separate exercise;
- ☐ posting of transactions to the sales ledger (assuming that this is not effected automatically following the entry of transactions);
- ☐ input of 'abnormal' transactions which may include items such as corrections of errors, contra entries between sales and purchase ledgers, adjustments to balances following agreement with customers or payments made to customers;
- ☐ possible interim aged analysis of debtors for management review or credit control follow up;
- ☐ *ad hoc* allocations of invoices against receipts and credit notes;
- ☐ general customer file maintenance;
- ☐ dealing with customer queries or disputes.

Purchase ledger

- input of purchase ledger cash payment batches (this may, of course, also be effected daily or just at the end of the period) and allocation against outstanding invoices;
- posting of transactions to the purchase ledger (assuming that this is not effected automatically following the entry of transactions);
- input of 'abnormal' transactions which may include items such as corrections of errors, contra entries between sales and purchase ledgers, adjustments to balances following agreement with suppliers or cash received from suppliers;
- *ad hoc* allocations of invoices against payments and credit notes;
- interim purchase ledger automatic payments run (for special prompt payments and discounts);
- reconciliation of purchase ledger accounts with supplier statements;
- general supplier file maintenance;
- dealing with supplier queries or disputes.

Nominal ledger

- possible interim updates of the nominal ledger with items posted to the sales and purchase ledgers;
- preparation and input of current period journals as and when they become available;
- general nominal master file maintenance.

General

- payment of *ad hoc* cheques;
- taking a separate 'week end' backup copy;
- it may also be advisable to run any utility provided to check the integrity of data, particularly if this is not performed as part of routine processing, such as during the ledger updates.

WHAT TO DO AT PERIOD END

The days leading up to the period end on each of the three ledgers are generally an active time, not least in the volume of paper which is to be produced by way of reporting from the ledgers. The following guidelines include the minimum which is likely to be required although, particularly in the case of reports, individual preferences and needs may dictate that far more is accomplished. Particular care should be taken to ensure that all reports which are designated as mandatory are printed before any final closure of a ledger period as most will not subsequently be available and the detail of transactions (and hence the 'audit trail') will be lost. Some systems will assist with this by the use of warning messages or even refusal to proceed with the end of period operation but, if none of this help is forthcoming, the onus will be on the user to plan accordingly.

The time which period end procedures may take also needs to be appreciated and it is not uncommon for at least a day to be spent closing the period on each of the ledgers. This is particularly worthy of note as, even in a multi-user environment, the system is likely to be unavailable during this time.

Sales ledger

- ☐ ensure that all transactions for the current period have been entered, including invoices, credit notes, adjustments and cash receipts;
- ☐ where possible, effect allocation of transactions where this has not already been done through cash or credit note entry;
- ☐ print the sales ledger control account and reconcile the movement on the account during the period with the batch control register;
- ☐ print end of period reports – the requirements will vary between organizations but will include, at the very least, the day book, a full ledger listing (ie including allocated transactions) and a list of customer balances, and probably the aged analysis of debtors;
- ☐ print, review and despatch customer statements;
- ☐ if end of VAT quarter, print VAT statistics (for VAT outputs);
- ☐ effect the period end routine to move the sales ledger into the next accounting period;
- ☐ if required, and if not in any case effected by the close of period routine, purge the ledger of allocated transactions, thus leaving only open items on the ledger (if this option is exercised, remember to print another sales ledger control account to confirm that the ledger balance has remained unchanged by the operation).

Purchase ledger

- ☐ run the final automated payments routine for the period, allowing sufficient time for review and amendment of the proposed payments before the close of period;
- ☐ ensure that all transactions for the current period have been entered; this includes invoices, credit notes, adjustments and cash payments outside of the automated payments procedures;
- ☐ where possible, effect allocation of transactions where this has not already been done through cash or credit note entry;
- ☐ print the purchase ledger control account and reconcile the movement on the account during the period with the batch control register;
- ☐ print end of period reports – the requirements will vary between organizations but will include, at the very least, the day book, a full ledger listing (ie including allocated transactions) and a list of supplier balances, and probably the aged analysis of creditors;
- ☐ if end of VAT quarter, print VAT statistics (for VAT inputs);

- ☐ effect the period end routine to move the purchase ledger into the next accounting period;
- ☐ if required, and if not in any case effected by the close of period routine, purge the ledger of allocated transactions, thus leaving only open items on the ledger (if this option is exercised, remember to print another purchase ledger control account to confirm that the ledger balance has remained unchanged by the operation).

Nominal ledger

- ☐ enter journals for the current period;
- ☐ enter cash and petty cash payments and receipts which have not otherwise been dealt with through the sales and purchase ledgers;
- ☐ determine accruals and enter them;
- ☐ update the nominal ledger, if this is not effected as part of the entry routine;
- ☐ print, at the very least, the trial balance report, a journal listing and a full nominal ledger listing;
- ☐ if required, transfer data to a spreadsheet or other external system for further manipulation;
- ☐ effect the period end routine to move the nominal ledger into the next period.

General

- ☐ perform end of period reconciliations as described in Chapter 12;
- ☐ take a 'period end' backup just before closing the period on each ledger, if not for each ledger, then at least for the nominal;
- ☐ if the integrity of ledger data is checked at no other time then this must be effected as part of the period end procedure although, in truth, it may be a bit late to find out that something is fundamentally wrong with the system. (Some systems will in any case include a data integrity check as part of routine processing, but the longer the time between integrity checks the greater the risk.)

Note the need for a 'period end' backup in the above requirements; this should be retained outside of the daily backup cycles until at least the end of the following period. Indeed, it can be worthwhile trying to retain the period end backup copies until at least the end of year, although this naturally depends on financial resources, particularly where relatively expensive media such as tape cartridge or removable hard disks are used. This gives you some safeguard if you have forgotten to take any of the vital end of period reports or, probably more likely, they have been mislaid. Note that it is not suggested that such backup copies are used instead of taking the reports at the proper time but rather as a safeguard.

WHAT TO DO AT YEAR END

The end of the financial year is frequently a fraught time for accountants and is frequently no less so for accounting systems. Not only are there the normal pressures of period end to worry about, but there is the likely need to keep the nominal ledger open for some weeks while year-end adjustments are made with the purchase and sales ledgers ploughing on into the next year. Many systems allow for the two years to be open concurrently, but it should be noted generally that systems tend to be under greater strain at these times because of increased activity (particularly in the nominal ledger), longer and more report runs and larger than normal file sizes. Among the tasks to be performed in addition to end of period activities at this time are the following.

Sales ledger

- □ print customer turnover and any other sales ledger statistics required;
- □ review of customer master file for dormant or otherwise redundant customer records which can be removed;
- □ effect write-offs or other adjustments which may be required.

Purchase ledger

- □ print supplier turnover and any other purchase ledger statistics required;
- □ review of supplier master file for dormant or otherwise redundant supplier records which can be removed;
- □ effect write-offs or other adjustments which may be required.

Nominal ledger

- □ determination and entry of journals to adjust errors made during the year;
- □ determination and entry of year-end accruals;
- □ revision of budget or forecast figures;
- □ transfer of balances on profit and loss accounts to reserves (if this is not effected automatically by the end of year routine).

General

- □ take a year-end backup to be retained at least until the audit of the accounts has been completed, thus providing an avenue to return to the end of year position if this is required *in extremis*.

CONCLUSION

While no two systems or organizations will be the same, the above at least provides a framework for the operation of a computerized accounting system. There are, of course, no 'right answers' and you will wish to draw up your own accounts timetable and supporting schedules in accordance with your particular requirements, taking into account the actual machinations of the software being used and the volume and timing of transactions. Having compiled a more detailed schedule, do not be tempted to keep it in your head; a simple tick list can work wonders when trying to ensure that all mandatory reports have been printed at the end of the period and helps to prevent the uncomfortable silence which sometimes follows when someone, perhaps an auditor, says, some months later: 'Can I just have a look at the day book for June please?'.

Above all, do not ignore the warning signs when events start to deviate from plan as catching up on a system which is moving ever further behind invariably leads to problems unless the underlying issues are acknowledged and tackled. The earlier this happens the better and, with a planned schedule of processing for the period, you should be in a good position to judge progress against an outside world in which customers continue to buy (you hope) and suppliers continue to supply; it should not be the accounting system itself which becomes the bottleneck.

12

Control and Security

FRAUD IS NOT THE ONLY PROBLEM

Those with a formal background in audit and accountancy will know only too well the fundamental importance of control and security when applied to accounting systems. However much disapproval there seems to be on the surface, one suspects that revelations on the subject of 'computer fraud' are found almost entertaining by many accountants. This is not only because of the natural interest in reading how the fraud was committed but also, if we must be honest, by deriving some comfort from the fact that it was perpetrated on someone else. Some frauds become very public knowledge; so public, in fact, that they fill quite a few column inches in the national press and some even get on TV. This is not a way in which anyone wishes to become famous but, behind every case of this nature, there is a system which is either insecure from fraudulent access or misuse or is so poorly controlled that the problem is not detected during the normal monitoring of events.

Fraud is not the only problem, however. There is a depressing number of things which can go awry with an accounting system (and particularly with a computerized accounting system) without any intentional malice aforethought. You could post the same batch of purchase invoices twice, for example; in the worst event this might then allow them also to be paid twice. You could suffer some file corruption on your disk so that the nominal ledger loses some of its transactions and hence no longer balances. You could, through a malfunction of some sort, end up with some transactions posted to the sales or purchase ledgers but not reflected on the nominal. A bug in the applications software might remove some transactions incorrectly during the end of period purge. All of these things, and more, *could* (and occasionally do) happen but, other than inconvenience, they will not escape the notice of the manager of a system in which proper controls are practised.

Managers without the benefit of an accountancy training often find control a difficult concept to grasp and, unless they are advised by someone who is better informed, will conclude that if everything appears to be working well, ie there are no obvious breakdowns or problems with the system, then there is little to worry about. If only life were so simple!

CONTROL

The concept of control

The underlying principle of control in an accounting system (or, for that matter, any other type of business system) is that you should not only be able to place absolute reliance upon each and every figure output from the system, but also that these outputs are the proper consequence of normal processing of the accounting information. Obviously, the processing and outputs stem largely from the information entered to the system and the integrity of such input data forms an important part of the overall control mechanisms.

To be able to feel so relaxed about things, attention must be given to the three principal elements of control.

- *Authorization*: Has all input been properly authorized before it is submitted to the computer?
- *Completeness*: Has everything been input and processed which should have been input and processed (once and once only)?
- *Accuracy*: Was the input and processing effected correctly?

You are not entirely alone in implementing these elements of control, the accounting software will almost certainly help apply the principle of accuracy by adopting batch control checks and validation of some of the input fields. It may even assist with the principle of completeness by, say, refusing to end a period if there are transactions which have been entered which have not yet been posted to the ledger although there would be little to be done if you had completely neglected to input a set of transactions. Where you will be alone, however, is on the question of authorization as this must be specific to each organization and set of circumstances; in a one-man business, for example, authorization will hardly apply.

Having proper control means also that you will be able successfully to trace the progress of a particular transaction through the system, from its original batch entry to the sales or purchase ledger to its consolidation into a balance on the nominal ledger some periods hence. This concept is frequently referred to as an 'audit trail', which should not really be a special feature of an accounting system (although it is frequently highlighted as such in marketing terms), but rather a natural product of the normal reporting structure of the system. It is for this reason that you should not be able to 'patch' (ie amend directly) a ledger transaction which has been found to be incorrect at some stage after posting to the ledger. An amendment of this nature would destroy the 'trail' of that transaction's progress through the system; the amendment should instead be effected by posting a separately identifiable amendment transaction(s), even if it means cancelling (by reversing out) the original transaction and then re-entering it.

In fact an acid test of an accounting system is for someone (and that someone is frequently an auditor) to point at a balance figure in, say, the nominal ledger and say: 'Show me how that figure is made up.' You will know that you are doing something wrong if you spend the next six months answering the query!

Remember, keep asking yourself these questions.

- Is it authorized?
- Is it complete?
- Is it accurate?

While those around may look curiously at you as you mutter this mantra you will be doing much for your own peace of mind in the future. This chapter cannot provide you with a control manual for your specific system and organization, but it can hopefully point you in the right direction of aspects which are likely to need attention. Your auditors should, of course, be able to provide detailed advice in this area and both you and they should be watchful that control systems, once set in place, do not lapse with time as other pressures build up or familiarity sets in.

Controls applied within the system

All accounting systems should have certain controls which are inbuilt. As these controls may or may not be documented it will not normally be sufficient to regard the computer system as a 'black box' and hope for the best but to include specific elements of controls in the testing arrangements advocated in Chapter 6. Internal controls are likely to relate to the following.

- The concept of batch control of input (note that this does not necessarily mean a batch update of the ledgers) has been introduced in Chapter 11. Batch control of transactions is one of the most effective elements in the manager's armoury and this topic is covered in more detail below.
- Validation of particular data fields in accordance with preset criteria, eg establishing that a date is in the correct format and is feasible, that a supplier account entered relates to an account held on the supplier file, and that nominal analysis is made to codes which are contained on the chart of accounts. As with any system, the earlier an exception is noted the better. For example, an invalid nominal code entered during invoice input is better noted and dealt with at this stage (while the source document is to hand and before the data has gone anywhere else in the system) rather than when the nominal ledger is updated some time later.
- With such items as the nominal analysis of purchase or sales invoices, it should not be possible to exit from the analysis process without having fully analysed the gross amount of the invoice in nominal terms (accepting, of course, that the VAT element will probably be dealt with automatically, just leaving the net amount to be analyzed).
- Journal type entry to the nominal ledger should contain safeguards which prevent unbalanced journals from being posted to the ledger. (Note that some systems enable unbalanced journals to be held in suspense until they are completed or cancelled at a later stage; this is fine as it is the *posting* of such journals which is to be avoided.)
- Any ledger update process should ensure that the items being posted in that run cannot be posted again in a subsequent run. Equally, it should not be possible accidentally to omit transactions from posting routines. The maxim 'once and once only' should apply.

- ☐ At some stage of processing (and some argue that it should be after each write operation to the ledger), the integrity of the complete ledger should be checked. This aspect is discussed later.

Batch control

From general experience, I have found that those with a formal accountancy training accept and apply batch control procedures over the input of transactions without question. This is not to imply that they are blinkered but rather that, to those with an understanding for the need and operation of control in an accounting system, batch control becomes second nature, a discipline which can be effected without the need for further fuss or ado.

The rub tends to come when it is encountered by those with a more general management (or at least less accounting oriented) background. When told to add up the values of transactions before entering them to the system they tend to say: 'but I thought the computer did the adding up for me'. The following paragraphs, therefore, are principally for those who align themselves with such a philosophy.

The underlying principle of batch control is that you should always approach a computer knowing exactly what it is that you are going to do and to come away with the absolute certainty that you have done it. Given that this is such a simple and laudable concept it is surprising that it is occasionally met with resistance by users of accounting systems, but such is life.

The batch control mechanism is to take a group of related transactions (eg purchase invoices, sales ledger receipts) and to sum their total value and record it. This is best done by means of a printed add listing which itemizes each constituent item in the batch as well as documenting the total. On commencement of input the system will generally prompt for the batch number (as allocated by you) and the batch value (as calculated by you). The transactions are then entered individually and the system records a running total of their values. At the end of input a report is normally produced by the system, and the running total is compared with the batch value entered at the start of input. If all has gone well then a 'batch reconciled' type of message is likely to appear on the batch input report; the more unfortunate occurrence of a 'batch control failure', while hardly good news, need not necessarily signal the end of the world, but it does mean that some action will need to be taken. In fact it is tempting to assume that batch control failures always relate to an error made during input and, while this is often the case, they can arise for the following reasons.

1. The original batch total was calculated incorrectly.
2. There may be an arithmetical discrepancy within one of the transactions. An example would be a purchase invoice on which the net and VAT totals did not add up to the gross figure shown. If the manual batch total had been calculated from the gross values but the input was effected through net and VAT figures (quite a likely scenario), the discrepancy would be shown up as a result of the batch control check.
3. A transaction had been entered incorrectly.

4. A transaction had been omitted.
5. A transaction had been entered more than once.
6. A transaction contained in the batch relates to a customer or supplier for which no master file record has been created.

The occurrence of a batch control failure should not be the cause of general pandemonium, alarm and despondency which sometimes ensues. Working logically through the possible causes of failure will invariably identify the cause(s); the action to be taken, however, may depend to some extent upon the facilities provided in the software. An error in the calculation of the batch total (as in 1. or 2. above) can be denoted by suitable annotation of the batch input report produced by the system. Input related errors (as in 3. to 5.) may be resolved by returning to the batch before it has been posted, by the entry of amendments or additional input in other batches or, in extreme cases where a number of errors have occurred, by cancelling the whole batch and starting again. Where a transaction has to be rejected (as in 6.) the batch input report and control register can be annotated accordingly and the item(s) entered in a supplementary batch when the relevant customer or supplier account records have been created.

The whole sequence of events will ideally be monitored and controlled through the operation of a batch control register, a document which is described in Chapter 7. Where circumstances permit, the operation of this register together with the make up and totalling of batches will be performed by someone other than the person making the input. In any event the originally calculated control total together with that produced by the batch input report and the cause and action taken in respect of any discrepancies should be documented. The batch control register itself can be used as a review document by those further up the supervisory ladder and, for example, it should be possible to reconcile the batch totals entered during an accounting period with the computer produced day book listings for that period.

Ledger integrity and other file tests

Accountants are naturally aware of the need, in a manual accounting system, to draw a trial balance to ensure the accounting integrity of entries which have been made according to the double entry convention, ie where the sum of debit entries equals those for credits. There is a tendency to think that there is no need for the same sort of check to be carried out in a computerized system, after all is not one of the advantages of such a system the fact that the accounts will always be in balance? Well, so they should in a good system but even though the ledger is held in a magnetic form and the rules of double entry are (or at least should be) enforced by the software there is every bit as much need to ensure that the file has integrity. Files can lose integrity because of:

- damage to the physical media upon which the file is resident, causing sectors which may prove to be unreadable or readable with random results;
- corruptions caused by, for example, dumping of memory contents at a point in time, perhaps as a result of a power cut or some similar form of physical malfunction;

- an incomplete set of records being added to the file as may occur, for example, if a ledger update process ended abnormally if the disk drive became full part of the way through the routine;
- where part of a file or records have been tampered with;
- through a fault in the applications software (hopefully the least likely cause).

Note that the integrity of files is not always at risk just when they are updated, although this is obviously the time at which they are most susceptible to something going wrong. For this reason many packages include the advice that a backup copy of data should be taken before a ledger posting routine is commenced.

Any of these occurrences could strike at any time and it is important, therefore, that the principal files in the system (ie ledgers, master files and day book transaction files) not only have a means of establishing that they have integrity but also that it is checked regularly and, even better, provide a means for the user to test the integrity on an *ad hoc* basis rather than waiting for the the next system test (which may be at the end of period) before finding out that there is something wrong.

The integrity of files should, ideally, be checked every time that they are updated but some consider that this adds too much of a processing overhead to operations. The dilemma is illustrated by, say, a batch of two invoices being added to a ledger containing 10,000 transactions. Is it reasonable to sum all 10,002 transactions after the update to see if the file still has integrity? Whatever the solution all accounting systems should contain some facility for checking the integrity of the principal files (and these must include the ledgers) even if it is present as a stand-alone utility which is run from outside the system. The facility should also extend to the recalculation, from the ledger transactions, of any memorandum balance figures such as are likely to be held on master files.

Controls applied around the system

Whatever controls are provided by the system itself there will still be much you can do to help matters by the general mode of operation. The actual controls implemented will inevitably depend upon the system being run, the staff resources available (both for operational work and for control) and the degree of importance which is attached to control procedures. Some of these include include the following.

Authorization of input

In principle, all input made to an accounts system should be approved (and evidenced as such by initial or signature). This may be effected on individual documents or on covering batch control sheets.

Marking of source documents

It should be possible to walk into an accounts office, pick up, say, a purchase invoice and be able to tell instantly whether or not that invoice has been posted to the ledger. If you cannot tell, then what is there to prevent it from being entered twice, or maybe not at all? Many organizations deal with this sort of requirement by devising a simple rubber stamp. The procedure involved is described in Chapter 7.

Division of responsibilities

A sound audit concept, but one which is frequently overlooked or forgotten in busy offices which are short of staff or where one person effectively makes all the input to the computer system. In effect, the key question is: 'Can one person do it all?' If the answer is 'yes' it should at least be recognized and perhaps compensating controls, such as a more rigorous management review of reports and evidencing of reconciliations, can be introduced.

Master file review

Control over the principal master files (ie the customer file in the sales ledger, the supplier file in the purchase ledger and the nominal chart of accounts) is of paramount importance, but the significance of this is often lost upon those with less experience. The addition, amendment or deletion of any master file data should be subject to a high level of control, with proper authorization and documentation, and should not be treated as an *ad hoc* exercise. The conflict between control and expediency is often highlighted by the facility, popular with many users and available in some systems, to be able to set up a new supplier or customer account 'on the fly' as purchase or sales invoice input is made. The control purists, however, would see such a facility as a bad thing, arguing that the ability to create new accounts in such a way makes control over master file operations more difficult to achieve.

Some systems provide a log of changes effected to master files and the review of such reports should be a defined part of routine control procedures. Even where such logs are not provided an occasional perusal of a full listing of customers and suppliers, preferably together with balance and turnover information, does not go amiss. Aside from the control consideration, such a review also gives an indication as to the level of dormant accounts which are being carried by the system and suitable candidates can be marked for deletion at the next opportunity.

Review of reports

A managerial review of the principal reports produced by the system can highlight not only problems relating to input but also indicate whether there are perhaps unreported errors within the system itself. Such an instance would be where the total of a list of customer or supplier balances did not agree with the total of a complete ledger listing indicating, perhaps, that the memorandum balance fields on the master files had become out of synchronization with the transaction files or that perhaps something even more serious has gone wrong in the form of a missing or duplicated transaction record. Similarly, a trial balance report which showed a misbalance would also be likely to indicate something going amiss within the system.

Exception reporting

The use of exceptions reports is a well-established technique for monitoring the health of operational systems. Exceptions reports are supposed to do precisely what the name implies, that is report upon items which, by some definition, are considered to be exceptional. Examples in an accounting environment would be:

- customer or supplier balances over a certain value;
- customer or suppliers with no account activity for a certain period of time (dormant accounts);
- transactions over a certain value;
- transaction entries which had been rejected during batch input.

Purchase ledger payments

Any point in a system through which cash payments can be generated must be liable to particularly strict controls and, in an accounting system, the payment of suppliers will be of greatest interest in this respect. In the simplest case, the purchase ledger listing or an aged creditors listing will be reviewed and the purchase invoices which are to be paid taken from the file. Cheques are then written in respect of these invoices and, the cheque number written on the invoices which are replaced in the file. The payments are written up in the cash book and posted to the purchase ledger at a later stage.

Many systems provide for 'automatic' payment facilities, ie facilities which scan the purchase ledger according to predefined criteria, select those invoices which are to be paid and then prepare postings and the means of payment, eg cheques or credit transfers. While such facilities are invaluable in a ledger of any size, it is essential that the potential for error or fraud is recognized and that pre-listings of transactions to be included in automated payments runs are obtained and reviewed before processing finally takes place.

Value stationery

Where the production of cheques forms part of the purchase ledger payment routines there will need to be special considerations applying, not only to the values printed on the cheques, but to the stationery itself. Apart from the obvious measure of storing such stationery securely, the principal problem relates to the wastage of cheques which is likely to occur with continuous stationery. Such wastage normally results either from:

- cheques being 'lost' in the tractor feed of the printer before printing commences, the tractor feed holding two or three cheques above the position of the print head so that printing actually commences on the third or fourth cheque – for this reason special printers, with tear-off bars, are often selected for cheque printing so that this form of wastage can be avoided;
- cheques being wasted in the alignment procedure.

The difficulty, of course, is that while the number of cheques initially lost in the tractor feed will remain constant, the number of attempts at printing cancelled cheques in the alignment process may justifiably vary between print runs. The correct procedures will include the maintenance of a control register listing sequences of cheque numbers so that completeness and continuity can be assured. The format would be something like:

Cheque	Numbers	Notes
Start	**End**	
900001	900003	Start of run of xx May 199x
900004	900005	Alignment xx May 199x
900006	900054	Payments made xx May 199x
900055	900057	Start of run of xx June 199x
900058	900061	Alignment xx June 199x
900062	900105	Payments made xx June 199x

Needless to say, cheques which are lost at the start of the run in a tractor feed must be cancelled by hand and evidence of all wasted cheques should be retained rather than disposed of.

Reconciliations

Reconciliations are activities which should be performed as a matter of routine rather than as an emergency measure when things have gone awry. The scope of reconciliations performed may vary with environments, but the following are likely to apply in all cases. The penalty for failing to carry out such reconciliations on a monthly (or, rather, accounting period) basis can be severe. With a monthly check, any discrepancies encountered can be viewed with the certainty that they must relate to the current period's processing which, given that all transactions will still be on file and events fresh in people's memories, will make the determination of the source, not to mention resolution, that much more simple. If such attention is not paid, the whole process becomes much more painful and, in all probability, exponentially more punitive in terms of effort.

The purpose of a reconciliation is to gain positive assurance that the accounting records accurately reflect the transactions which have been processed. It is not sufficient to state (or even believe) that 'computers never make mistakes': they can and sometimes do (although usually in connection with a hardware or software problem) and, even if they did not, human beings are more than capable of making plenty.

Depending upon the environment, a reconciliation should be evidenced by signature or initials and, where applicable, the actual reconciliation calculation should be shown. In this way, there can be no doubt as to whether a particular reconciliation has been performed or not and, perhaps more importantly, it is very clearly somebody's responsibility to have carried it out.

Some of the more important reconciliations follow.

Sales and nominal ledgers

A fundamental check is to ensure that the balance of the sales ledger is equal to the debtors control account held in the nominal. This reconciliation should be easily evidenced by taking a control account listing from the sales ledger system and comparing the total of this with the debtors control account in the nominal ledger. They should be identical. If they are not, perhaps one of the following has happened:

- if the system permits it (and not all do) nominal journals have been posted directly to the debtors control account;
- there has been a breakdown in processing between the update of the sales ledger and the update of the nominal ledger such that transactions have been posted to one of the ledgers more than once or perhaps not at all;
- there is a corruption contained within one of the ledger files.

The last two in particular are not good news and, depending upon circumstances, may necessitate a restoration from a backup copy taken before the discrepancy and the reprocessing of all subsequent transactions. That is one very good reason why reconciliations should not be more than a month apart!

While effecting this reconciliation it is also worthwhile quickly checking the totals printed on the sales ledger listing, the listing of customer balances and any other reports (eg ageing analysis) which purport to give a ledger total. They should all be identical.

Purchase and nominal ledgers

Exactly the same principle applies with regard to the purchase ledger total and the creditors control account held in the nominal ledger.

These reconciliations are the most fundamental which can be performed in an integrated accounts system and their failure can be viewed with concern. All further processing should be suspended until the matter has been satisfactorily resolved.

Batch update reconciliation

Proper maintenance of a batch control register enables the following reconciliation to be easily performed:

Balance b/f from last month

Plus	:	Invoice batches
Minus	:	Credit note batches
Plus/Minus	:	Adjustments
Minus	:	Receipts (SL)/payments (PL)
Plus	:	Payments (SL)/receipts (PL)
Equals	:	Current ledger balance

This gives an assurance that, for example, no batch has been entered twice, nor has any been omitted. Failure of this reconciliation should be viewed bleakly; the best thing that could have happened is a mistake in the batch control register, the worst hardly bears thinking about. Some systems can aid matters further by enabling a reconciliation to be performed easily between the total of each transaction type and a day book type of listing.

Cash book reconciliation

The maintenance of a manual cash book should facilitate the reconciliation between this and the nominal account used for the bank account (sometimes called cash book control). As noted in Chapter 7, one of the problems with a computerized system is that cash items are entered into the system through all three ledgers and hence their control during the accounting period can be difficult. This end of period reconciliation, therefore, gives assurance that all the cash items have been entered correctly (at least in terms of monetary values) and that they have ended up in the correct account (at least as far as one side of the double entry is concerned) in the nominal ledger.

Obviously, where more than one bank account is maintained, the equivalent reconciliation can be effected for all.

Bank reconciliation

In general, the bank reconciliation (ie the reconciliation between the cash book balance at period end and that shown on the bank statement) is outside the realms of the computerized accounting system although some systems, particularly those which concentrate on cash book features, do incorporate facilities to assist with this. From the viewpoint of the accounting system, the important thing is that the cash book balance is in agreement with the relevant account in the nominal ledger. If, as a result of carrying out the bank reconciliation, the cash book balance is found to be incorrect (eg some items paid directly by the bank were omitted from the cash book) it will be necessary also to make the relevant entries into the ledger systems and to repeat the cash book reconciliation as detailed above.

Master file integrity

Most systems will provide for a simple listing of balances by individual account, these balances being quite likely to be produced from memorandum fields held on the relevant master file rather than by derivation of the current balance from the transactions held on the ledger. It is, therefore, worthwhile to check occasionally that the total of such listings agrees with the ledger control account and, therefore, with the total of a ledger listing and, for sales and purchase ledgers, with the relevant control account maintained in the nominal ledger.

SECURITY

The concept of security

'Security' is a word which can strike fear into the heart of a computer manager and, with the scare stories which sometimes appear to be endemic in the press, perhaps it is right that such an area should be viewed with caution. Security is, however, a relative matter and must fit in easily with the operation of a system. A large accounting system which is accessed by a number of users and is resident on a machine also used for other applications will obviously be at greater risk than a stand-alone system which is operated by one user in a small office.

The threats to accounting data are more severe than many imagine. The predominant fear tends to be of fraud committed by a member of the accounting department staff, but an equally depressing prospect is that of theft, or at least misappropriation, of data. The ledger systems, by their very nature, contain information which is the quintessence of an organization's operation. Customer lists, customer turnovers, sales figures, margins, supplier discounts and profitability are all available even to the less experienced eye and the damage that such information could do if placed in the hands of an aggressive or unscrupulous competitor is unthinkable.

In the days of manual ledgers, this information was dispersed around a number of bulky documents or cards and it would have been difficult for someone to walk off with them all and also obvious once they had gone. This is not so with computerized systems; copying the data files to a diskette which can be slipped into the pocket is all that may be needed and nobody will be any the wiser that such a copy has been taken. Just think of the implications of this happening and then think of the number of people who would have the opportunity to carry out such an operation. That is why the subject of security looms so large in the minds of accounting system managers.

Security of access to systems

The security of systems has become of increasing concern in recent years, particularly as the concepts of connectivity and open systems have been directed towards an easier sharing and transfer of data, not to mention the less savoury and insidious spreading of viruses.

The most common means for securing access employed in accounting systems is the use of password protection at one or more of the following levels:

- ☐ on initial boot (ie a password implemented by the operating environment, particularly found in networked or multi-user systems);
- ☐ on entry of a user identifier to the accounting system (again for multiple access systems);
- ☐ on selection of a particular menu option within the accounting system;
- ☐ occasionally, on selection of a particular function within a routine.

The effectiveness of passwords as a means of control over access to systems and/or functions has been debated at length in computer literature. Suffice to say that, although not perfect, password protection is generally better than none at all and it will at least deter the casual or inexperienced 'intruder', whether he is malevolent or just curious.

The precise usage of passwords is likely to be dictated principally by the applications software and passwords will need to be designed within the constraints which will apply. Some general rules are:

- if possible, use at least six characters for the password;
- try not to use proper nouns, etc;
- change passwords occasionally and certainly when a user of the accounting system leaves or where any unauthorized use of the system is suspected;
- ensure that the top level (or 'master' or 'system') password is not solely entrusted to one person; if necessary, keep the current passwords in a sealed envelope in a secure location in case of unforeseen events.

Remember that, however securely you operate the password procedures, it may still be possible for passwords to be 'cracked' by those with sufficient time and expertise. Indeed the need for passwords may be circumvented by going direct to the raw data files. This opens up a further area of concern.

Security of data

Whatever safeguards are implemented within the applications software itself the alert manager will always be on the lookout for the possibility of data being accessed outside the software, ie through the operating system. Accounting system data files are no different from those of any other system in that they reside as identifiable files on disk and these files may be viewed, albeit in a raw form, and even edited through operating system or other utility programs. They can also be copied on to portable magnetic media so that they can be looked at in the privacy of another installation. From this viewpoint, even the operation of taking a backup copy of data has its dangers as proper security needs also to be applied to the various copies of the data which exist outside the computer and, of course, the unauthorized taking of a backup copy needs also to be guarded against.

The finer points of security will depend upon the precise installation and also the perceived level of threat, but the following guidelines are likely to apply in many instances.

- Access to the operating system should be closely controlled and limited to, say, a 'Systems Manager', and his reserve. With such access, the world is open to anyone who wishes to browse through, edit or copy your data files. Control over access can often be effected by front-end menus which define what facilities are available to each user of the system.
- File editing utilities (and any other utilities which enable files to be inspected or copied) should, as far as possible, be removed from the immediate environment. This cannot always be totally achieved because many operating systems contain such utilities as built-in commands which only reinforce the need not to permit unauthorized access to the operating system. When, and if, any such utilities are required they can be brought to the machine through the means of a floppy disk or held in a form which controls their access.
- In hard disk systems, the floppy disk drive is often the Achilles' heel of security; whatever controls are implemented on the hard disk, these can often be circumvented by access (or even booting) through the floppy drive.
- Where accounting systems are on computers which are shared with other applications, be alert to the possibility of users of these applications gaining access to accounting system files.

- Where the computer has links to remote systems, review the likely security implications. The proclivities of hackers have by now aroused sufficient media interest for everyone to be aware of the dangers relating to computers with external communications installed.

The above portrays a gloomy scenario, which is possibly why so many managers are blissfully unaware of the dangers involved. Rather than go grey worrying about security (and it is quite easy to do so), at least try to remember the following tips.

- Be conscious of the risks and include these risks in your management planning.
- Review security arrangements periodically as a formal exercise.
- Ensure that staff are made aware of the importance with which security is viewed and of the need to report any breaches.
- Be on your guard when people unconnected with your organization (or even those within your organization but outside the accounts department), such as engineers, training personnel and programmers have access to the computer on which your accounts system is run. This is not to say, of course, that you should regard all such people as criminals, but remember that it is you who has most to lose should they make a mistake and you should at least take a backup copy before they start work.
- Do not countenance the downloading of *ad hoc* files on to any computer on which the accounting system is run nor the copying on of files from unauthorized floppy diskettes. There are enough problems with which to contend without adding the threat of viruses to the list.

The computer hardware and software manufacturers have quickly latched on to users' general concerns in the field of security and there are now many products which provide help in this direction. These range from front-end (and password protected) user shells through data encryptors to computers which purport to be physically inviolate from unauthorized access. These may be taking a sledgehammer to crack the proverbial nut for some but, where security matters, they will be worth their cost for the peace of mind which ensues.

Taking security (backup) copies

The concepts of taking backup copies of data are well-established and there are many computing textbooks which detail approaches such as the 'grandfather – father – son' cyclic utilization of backup media. Most accounting software manuals will offer guidance on the files which need to be included in the backup operation and the rationale of the backup procedure.

As well as these routine (and probably daily) backups, however, the user of an accounting system will also normally wish to take additional 'point in time' copies of data as an additional safeguard against operating problems or just because of the need to return to a point to obtain a report which had been lost or forgotten. Naturally, the willingness to take, and to retain, additional backup copies will be dictated by:

- the cost of the backup media;

- the time taken to perform the backup operation;
- the inconvenience (and potential risk) of a restoration of a backup copy and the subsequent restoration of current data.

Among the times at which additional backup copies may be required are:

- before any ledger update;
- before a purchase ledger automated payments run;
- before the closure of a nominal ledger period;
- before the closure of the year on the nominal ledger;
- before any major master file deletion process;

and no doubt others exist according to local circumstances and preferences. Remember that, if a corruption occurs in your files and is undetected for a few days (perhaps there has been no ledger posting in this time for example), your routine backup copies are all likely to contain this corruption. This is when the retention of an older backup copy, taken at a point when the data is known to be sound, such as period end, can be a life (well, at least a sanity) saver.

One of the most vital documents in an accounting system (and, for that matter, any system of importance) is the backup register, which was introduced in Chapter 7.

In addition to the normal items to be recorded in this register (as detailed in Chapter 7), it is also useful in an accounting system to note the last event which has taken place before the backup copy was made. For example, this could be: 'entry of sales ledger invoice batch No 123'; even better would be the last event on each of the three ledgers. In this way, should the need to restore from a particular backup copy arise, re-entry and reprocessing can commence with the minimum of fuss and no need for questions such as 'now, let me think, did I do a backup before or after I posted that cash?' Remember that the person restoring from the backup copy (who may of course be you) need not necessarily be the person who took the backup, hence the need for punctilious documentation.

As a final thought, if you suspect your data files of being corrupt (as well you might, for example, if a hardware error occurs part of the way through a ledger posting routine), by all means take a backup copy of the data (in case, for example, the hard disk needs to be changed or reformatted), but whatever you do, *do not* overwrite a normal backup copy in doing so. In my experience, the guilty reaction of those who do not regularly take backup copies of data is immediately to do so when a problem has occurred, often overwriting their only course of salvation.

13

Looking for Information

A POSITIVE NOTE

It is appropriate to end this book on a positive note. We started out by saying what could go wrong with a computerized accounting system and it was only right to sound a warning to those who thought that responsibility for the quality of accounting information was transferred elsewhere merely by the purchase of a package. A good accounting system should, however, mean so much more than just getting the sales, purchase and nominal ledgers operative and up to date. Admittedly, there will be some who look little further than this, perhaps just requiring also that the work for the quarterly VAT return is made easier whereas there may be others who would be grateful just to get up to date!

If, however, you are able to climb above the tasks of day-to-day accounting you may be able to catch a glimpse of a picture in which the information you have captured and used in your accounting system becomes vested with wider properties. Indeed, it is a shame that many managers see the computerization of the accounting function as an end in itself rather than as a starting point for getting more information about the business. The more enlightened accounting systems deal with management (in its widest sense), as well as financial and accounting requirements, and they also provide general management information, for example in terms of marketing. To illustrate the point at the simplest level, the ageing analysis of debtors can be used as an example of information which can be achieved easily through the use of a system but which would be far more difficult to replicate by manual methods. The potential is there but relatively few take advantage of it.

As noted, there is still room for improvements in attitudes but, in an increasingly competitive world, it would be a strange organization indeed which did not seek to gain the maximum benefit from the information at its disposal, particularly if there is no additional penalty incurred in the capture of that information. To some extent the problem relates to an historic (or perhaps traditional) view towards information, and the managers who have grown up with discretely implemented systems perhaps become ingrained with the view that there is 'a personnel system there, an accounts system there, a production control system there' and so on, compartmentalizing these without thinking of the synergic effects of such data.

Many people now pay lip-service to the concepts of management information, but that does not necessarily mean that they do anything about it. Here are some easy questions. How many customers did you have last year? How many new customers have you gained this year? How many of last year's customers are no longer customers this year? Easy enough questions you may think, but I wonder how many are able quickly to answer them. Yet the answers could be gleaned from any self-respecting sales ledger (eg by interrogation of the customer file or by looking at turnover reports) without too much of a problem. Of course such questions may lead on to other, less comfortable, queries such as *why* have those customers disappeared but at least you are in possession of some concrete facts and have a means of cross-checking with the data perhaps provided by the sales force.

GETTING AT YOUR DATA

Even if there is a willingness to get to grips with the potential, and possibly untapped, information within a system there may be an effective barrier placed by the accounting software itself. Certainly if this software provides only limited interrogation or analysis facilities and there is no other 'user friendly' way of accessing data files the exercise is likely to be difficult, or even impossible.

There is, however, a growing trend to present a more uniform and informative interface to users and the use of various standard data formats has assisted with this. Such data formats commonly allow meaningful access to the files by third party packages and, providing that the file structures can be comprehended, there may be scope for some analysis which is not available within the system itself. Additionally, the growing importance of structured query languages (SQLs) and accounting databases in the microcomputer environment is also likely to contribute to the user's cause in this respect. Another increasingly used avenue is the transfer of accounting data into a spreadsheet system where further work on the data can be carried out.

Many writers of accounting systems have recognized this need and have addressed it, with varying degrees of success, through the incorporation of a report writer within or alongside the main system. As the term implies, a report writer enables the user to define additional reports which may be required from the system without having to go back to the software house and ask for an amendment. The user is guided as to the file and field names required and, within certain constraints, will be able to design a report to his specification. Once specified, this report definition can be saved and executed at any time thereafter, thereby effectively adding to the number of reporting options available from the system. Report writers were originally incorporated in many systems to enable customized versions of the profit and loss and balance sheet reports to be produced but the generalization of their use has been a bonus to users and the more sophisticated will allow reports to be produced conditionally, eg list all customers with the post code KT.

Access to data files, other than through the formal applications software, is of course a threat to security which should be considered very carefully before it is countenanced. There are few auditors who would be impressed by you demonstrating an ability to 'patch' a raw data file through the use of a utility, and any software tools which permit accounting data files to be inspected, interrogated or, most importantly, amended should be subject to the most strict controls over use. In any event, it is rarely advisable to access a live system file, other than through the applications software itself; the possibilities for corruption, whether deliberate or inadvertent, make this too much of a risk. It is far safer to take a copy of the file(s) required into another area of disk and thus to conduct the interrogation well away from any live data.

Where you require further information from your data and you are unable or unwilling to 'do it yourself', or would in any case prefer the facility to be available from within the mainstream system, you will probably have to ask for an amendment to be made to your software. The pros and cons of amending systems were discussed in Chapter 5 and it may often be advisable, if possible, to have additional reports, etc available as separate utilities outside the main system so that you do not become precluded from any general upgrades which may be made to the core software from time to time.

WHAT SORT OF INFORMATION MIGHT YOU WANT?

What sort of additional information might you want which may not be satisfied by the normal accounting processing? While there is no universal answer, and much may in any case depend upon the sophistication of the nominal ledger in operation, a good place to illustrate the sort of information which may be available, and which might not be supplied by the mainstream system, is in the sales ledger.

There is, for example, a growing realization that the sales ledger, or rather the customer master file containing details of customer accounts, forms an invaluable base for direct marketing. This file has a number of advantages.

First, it needs to be maintained, at least for credit customers, to enable the sales ledger to function. In general, at least the customer's name and address would be held but there are also likely to be other contact details such as:

- contact name;
- telephone number;
- telex number;
- fax number.

The above fields are, of course, likely to relate principally to contacts in accounts departments (or more specifically in the purchase ledger department), but more advanced systems, or at least those which are designed on a database principle, are also likely to incorporate facilities for other contacts, such as those required by the marketing or sales force.

Secondly, the customer file may also contain other useful accounting information such as:

- current balance;
- turnover in current year;

- turnover in a number of previous years;
- date of last transaction;
- date account was set up.

Before getting too carried away on the marketing side, however, a couple of things need to be remembered about the general nature of customer master files.

- Only actual customers are held on them; ie only organizations which have actually bought something (and that on credit) will be held on the file. Thus, even potential customers, who make enquiries but do not buy, will not generally be recorded.
- Unless the file is managed carefully, it will tend to accumulate dormant accounts, ie those customers who have not been active for some time, perhaps because they are no longer in business or because they made only the one *ad hoc* purchase.

Nevertheless, there are no people more important to a business than its customers and the more which can be done to monitor and analyze their patterns and levels of trading the better. Such information is often readily available by looking at the customer file from a different viewpoint. In fact the customer and sales ledger files could yield some very interesting facts in addition to the basic ledger maintenance data. Among those which come to mind are these:

- 'Best customers' reporting, ie reporting of customers in decreasing order of turnover for the current and past years. In some systems this could be refined to report turnover by months or quarters and even to compare these with the same periods in the preceding year.
- 'New' accounts reporting; eg how many new accounts in specified period, turnover with new accounts as against that with existing customers?
- 'Dormant' customers reporting, ie those customer accounts with no activity for a specified period of time; eg what percentage of the customer file is taken up by customers with whom you have not traded in the past two years?
- Customer statistics by various types of category, such as sales representative, geographical area, customer type, source of origin of customer, etc.
- Exceptions reports, such as credit limit excesses, listing customers whose current balance (and, if applicable, value of sales orders in progress) exceed their specified credit limits.
- The following type of statistics may be produced by customer and for the whole ledger:
  - number of invoices in a given period;
  - average value of invoices in a given period;
  - average days taken to pay invoices.
- For sales ledgers which are linked with stock or invoicing systems, analysis of sales by product by customer by period (by quantity and/or value) may be possible. On a related front, figures such as average selling price per product could be achieved and even gross profit and margin by customer may be made available if suitable cost prices can be linked for each sale.

- An interesting rider to the ageing analysis of debtors is to assign probabilities of payment against invoices which are old; eg 75 per cent probability if over three months, 50 per cent if over six months, 25 per cent if nine months or older. These probabilities can then be used to provide an adjusted debtors total with a guidance as to a bad debt provision.

Not all the above information may be readily available in all systems and, in some, it could not easily be made so. It is, however, the concept which is important: to get into the way of thinking of what *more* can I get from my data? In the vast majority of systems, a reasonable amount of base data is already being held which could almost certainly be made into useful information. Just look at the list (and doubtless you can think of more to add to it) and ask yourself if any of it would be useful, if not to you, then to someone else in your organization. Similar concepts could be applied to the purchase ledger and, for that matter, to any other system under your control.

OTHER DIRECTIONS

Much of the benefit of accounting systems can be gained from the integration with other types of software and there is a growing trend not only for integration between different modules within a package (and even between modules of other packages) but also for integration with 'foreign' types of software. This was noted in Chapter 4 and prime examples include:

- spreadsheet and modelling systems;
- word processing;
- desktop publishing;
- graphics software;
- database systems.

The above possibilities mean that there is very little excuse for poor presentation of accounts and there is much to be gained, not least in terms of communication with non financial staff, by using some of the techniques mentioned above. It has long been recognized, for example, that some people respond far better to financial information presented in a pictorial form (eg as a pie chart or pictogram) than in words and figures and there are now opportunities to produce just such a form of output with a minimum amount of additional work. The increasing simplicity of communications products and, indeed, the general trend towards connectivity between hardware, operating system and applications environments also means that the possibilities of combining and consolidating data from a variety of remote sources are becoming greatly extended. In effect, the boundaries of the accounting system are becoming wider and wider.

Some modern software products now incorporate facilities to build files of a seemingly mixed format so that word processed text, a graph created by a modelling system and data from a data file (eg from an accounts package) can be intermixed. The use of different fonts and shading when printing, and the possibility of colour, means that the traditional presentation of tightly packed spreadsheet figures produced on a fading dot matrix printer now looks dated, to say the least.

All this sounds very exciting, and it is worth considering that, in the 1990s, merely to run a successfully computerized accounting system, which at one time would have been regarded as an achievement in itself, should really be looked upon as a starting point. The days are long gone when accounts was a function which could whirr and hiss away in the twilight hours of computing time for the benefit of a few introspective people buried deep in the bowels of an organization.

In essence, accounting systems should now be viewed as: the *start*, not the *finish*; a *part*, not a *whole*; and the *future*, not the *past*!

Good luck!

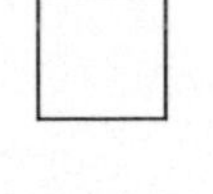

Index